KEY IDEAS IN TRUSTS LAW

This book provides an in-depth and easy-to-understand account of a subject that students often find dauntingly difficult to master.

The opening chapter sets out some definitions of what a trust is, and goes on to clearly explain the history of trusts law and how both trusts law and the roles played by trusts have changed over time. Different types of trust (trusts for persons, charitable and non-charitable purpose trusts, express trusts, constructive trusts, and resulting trusts) are explored in detail over the following two chapters. The fourth chapter sets out the law on when someone will commit a breach of trust and what remedies will be available when such a breach is committed; the obscure and intimidating terminology that affects this area of law is explained and made easy to use. A concluding chapter explores the harms caused by trusts law, particularly through its use to store wealth in tax havens abroad, and considers possibilities for reforming the law to mitigate those harms.

With references to almost 150 books and articles, and almost 150 cases, this book will save students a huge amount of time in terms of developing a sophisticated knowledge of the past, present and potential futures of trusts law, both in England & Wales and across the world, as well as the academic and judicial debates that surround this area of law.

Key Ideas in Law: Volume 4

Key Ideas in Law

Series Editor: Nicholas J McBride

Hart Publishing's series *Key Ideas in Law* offers short, stimulating introductions to legal subjects, providing an opportunity to step back from the detail of the law to consider its broader intellectual foundations and ideas, and how these work in practice.

Written by leading legal scholars with great expertise and depth of knowledge, these books offer an unparalleled combination of accessibility, concision, intellectual breadth and originality in legal writing.

Each volume will appeal to students seeking a concise introduction to a subject, stimulating wider reading for a course or deeper understanding for an exam, as well as to scholars and practitioners for the fresh perspectives and new ideas they provide.

Recent titles in this series:

For the complete list of titles in this series, see www.bloomsbury.com/uk/series/key-ideas-in-law/

Key Ideas in Trusts Law

Nicholas J McBride

·H A R T·
OXFORD · LONDON · NEW YORK · NEW DELHI · SYDNEY

HART PUBLISHING

Bloomsbury Publishing Plc

Kemp House, Chawley Park, Cumnor Hill, Oxford, OX2 9PH, UK

1385 Broadway, New York, NY 10018, USA

29 Earlsfort Terrace, Dublin 2, Ireland

HART PUBLISHING, the Hart/Stag logo, BLOOMSBURY and the Diana logo are
trademarks of Bloomsbury Publishing Plc

First published in Great Britain 2023

Copyright © Nicholas J McBride, 2023

Nicholas J McBride has asserted his right under the Copyright, Designs and
Patents Act 1988 to be identified as Author of this work.

A catalogue record for this book is available from the British Library.

A catalogue record for this book is available from the Library of Congress.

Library of Congress Control Number: 2023933437

ISBN:	PB:	978-1-50993-869-8
	ePDF:	978-1-50993-871-1
	ePub:	978-1-50993-870-4

Typeset by Compuscript Ltd, Shannon

To find out more about our authors and books visit www.hartpublishing.co.uk.
Here you will find extracts, author information, details of forthcoming events
and the option to sign up for our newsletters.

For Bill S and Rob S
migliori fabbri

CONTENTS

1

Foundations

1. DEFINITIONS

Let's begin our exploration of the law of trusts with a few different definitions of what a trust is:

'I should define a trust in some such way as the following – When a person has rights which he is bound to exercise upon behalf of another or for the accomplishment of some particular purpose he is said to have those rights in trust for that other or for that purpose and he is called a trustee. It is a wide vague definition, but the best that I can make.' (Maitland 1936, 44).

'For the purposes of this Convention, the term "trust" refers to the legal relationships created – *inter vivos* or on death – by a person, the settlor, when assets have been placed under the control of a trustee for the benefit of a beneficiary or for a specified purpose.

A trust has the following characteristics –

(a)   the assets constitute a separate fund and are not part of the trustee's own estate;

(b)   title to the trust assets stands in the name of the trustee ...;

(c)   the trustee has the power and the duty, in respect of which he is accountable, to manage, employ or dispose of the assets in accordance with the terms of the trust and the special duties imposed upon him by law.'

(Hague Trusts Convention 1985, Art 2)

'A trust ... is a fiduciary relationship with respect to property, arising from a manifestation of intention to create that relationship and subjecting the person who holds title to the property to duties to deal with it for the benefit of charity or for one or more persons, at least one of whom is not the sole trustee.' (Restatement 3d, Trusts, §2 (2003))

These definitions allow us to make the following points about trusts:

SUBJECT MATTER

The Hague Convention and the Third Restatement of Trusts (drawn up by the American Law Institute) both refer to the subject matter of a trust as being 'property', while Maitland refers to it as being 'rights'. Maitland's view is wider: not all rights are property rights. My right that you not punch me in the face is not a property right. Nor is my publisher's contractual right that I get this book finished by my deadline. Maitland's view also seems to be better. This is because it is possible to hold contractual rights on trust for another (*Fletcher* v *Fletcher* (1844) 5 Hare 67).

However, where Tom holds a contractual right against Dan on trust for Ben, the trust behaves in a peculiar way. If Dan commits a breach of contract, Tom will be able (and will, indeed, be bound) to sue Dan for compensation for the losses suffered by *Ben* as a result of Dan's breach: *Lloyds* v *Harper* (1880) 16 Ch D 290. (Tom will then hold the damages recovered on trust for Ben.) This is not what happens if Tom holds *property* on trust for Ben. If Dan wrongfully damages the property, Tom will only be able to recover compensation for the damage to the property, and not for the losses that Ben personally suffers as a result of the property being damaged. This was a problem in *Shell UK Ltd* v *Total UK Ltd* [2011] QB 86. UKOP held an oil pipeline on trust for Shell. Due to Total's fault, the pipeline blew up, and Shell suffered millions of pounds in business losses as a result. UKOP could only sue for compensation for the damage to the pipeline, and could not recover anything for Shell's losses. The Court of Appeal held that Shell could sue for compensation *in their own right* for the loss that it had suffered as a result of the pipeline being blown up. The decision has been criticised on the basis that the court's decision assumed that Shell had some kind of interest in the pipeline that entitled them to sue Total for blowing it up, when in fact – and in line with the above definitions – the only right Shell had under the trust was that UKOP administer the pipeline for their benefit (Edelman 2013, 72–74; Swadling 2019a, 103–10).

If Ben's rights under a trust are not property rights (though, as we will see, they are capable of affecting third parties to the trust), then if Ben's rights can themselves be held on trust then that would provide an additional demonstration that it is wrong to think that only property rights can be held on trust for another. And indeed, Ben's rights *can* be held on trust, so that Tom can hold rights on trust for Ben, and Ben can hold his rights under that trust on trust for Cat. The trust that exists between Ben and Cat is known as a *sub-trust*.

It used to be thought that if there were no material distinction between the trust existing between Tom and Ben, and the trust between Ben and Cat, then Ben would simply drop out and Tom would hold directly on trust for Cat. The better view appears to be now that Ben stays in place with the result that if Ben declares that he holds his rights under the Tom-Ben trust on trust for Cat, no direct trust between Tom and Cat arises: *Nelson* v *Greening & Sykes (Builders) Ltd* [2007] EWCA Civ 1358, [57]. This is fortunate for Cat. The Law of Property Act 1925, s 53(1)(c) says that if Tom holds rights on trust for Ben and Ben wants to make it so that Tom holds those rights on trust for Cat and not for Ben, then Ben will only be able to do this in writing. But if Ben stays in place when he declares that he holds his rights under the Tom-Ben trust on trust for Cat, Ben's declaration will *not* have the effect of destroying the Tom-Ben trust and creating a new trust between Tom and Cat. Ben's declaration will therefore be perfectly effective even if he made it orally and not in writing.

THE TRUSTEE

The trustee of a trust is a right-holder but a trustee is not like other right-holders. By this, I don't just mean that they are bound to exercise those rights on behalf of someone else or for some purpose – as the above definitions indicate – but that they hold those rights in a different capacity from other right-holders, and in particular in a completely different capacity from someone who holds rights *beneficially*.

As William Swadling points out, there are five *different* ways 'in which the common law recognises that rights can be held': '(1) outright/beneficially/absolutely; (2) as security for the performance of an obligation; (3) as executor/administrator of a deceased's estate; (4) as administrator of an insolvent estate; and (5) as a trustee' (Swadling 2016, 953). Suppose then that I am the absolute owner of a bag of gold coins, and I declare that I hold the bag of coins on trust for you. One way of analysing what I have done is that I have taken the rights I have over the coins as their owner and encumbered them with rights that you will hold against me. But on the view advanced here, I have done more than this. I have changed *the way* I am holding the rights that I originally had over the coins: I am no longer holding them as a beneficial owner but as a trustee. The Hague Convention on Trusts goes some way to recognising this in the above definition when it says that trust assets 'are not part of the trustee's own estate', as does s 2 of the Trusts (Jersey) Law 1984, which specifies that property held on trust is not owned by the trustee 'in the [trustee's] own right'.

So in what capacity does the trustee hold the rights that they hold on trust? The best view is that they hold them as an office-holder (see Penner 2020). The rights are, in a sense, not attached to the trustee but to the office that the trustee occupies. So if Tom is a trustee and Tom goes bankrupt, Tom's creditors will not be able to access any funds that he holds on trust to pay off the debts he owes them because those funds don't (in a sense) belong to Tom, but to the office that he occupies: Insolvency Act 1986, s 283(3)(a). This 'asset-partitioning' or 'ring-fencing' effect of a trust is, as we will see, a major reason for people's seeking to argue that funds are held on trust. However, it would be a mistake to think that trusts exist to have this effect; trusts have this effect because trustees are office-holders.

The fact that Tom is an office-holder also explains why if he dies or retires, the trust does not die. Tom's death or retirement means that the office that he occupied is now vacant, but the office still exists and it must be filled with a new trustee. If one cannot be found, the Public Trustee or a trust company can be appointed to take on the job: Public Trustee Act 1906; Trustee Act 1925, s 42. The courts also have the power under s 41 of the Trustee Act 1925 to dismiss Tom from his office and appoint a replacement if he 'lacks capacity to exercise his functions as trustee'. Consistently with the position adopted here, C Reinold Noyes observes that 'When a trustee is removed for cause the [trust] property is not taken away from him. He is taken away from the property' (Noyes 1936, 469). The trust assets go with the trustee's office, not with the trustee.

BOUND

All of the above definitions make it clear that a trustee is not free to do what they like with the subject matter of the trust. Instead, they must apply it – in accordance with the terms of the trust – on behalf of certain persons or purposes. A trust which does not bind the trustee in this way is not a trust at all. So in *Armitage* v *Nurse* [1998] Ch 241, Millett LJ confirmed that a term in the trust instrument that exempted the trustee from liability for actual fraud would be invalid. Such a term would leave the trustee free to do whatever they liked with the trust assets and thereby offend against the idea that there is an 'irreducible core of obligations' that a trustee must be subject to if there is to be a trust (at 253).

Robert Stevens sometimes seems to suggest that *whenever* Ben has a right (from whatever source) that Tom exercise his rights over an asset for Ben's benefit, then Tom can be said to hold that asset on trust for Ben (see, for example, Stevens 2012, 925). However, as Stevens would be the first to admit (see McFarlane & Stevens 2010, 12–15) this is somewhat overstated. There are situations where Ben has a right that Tom deploy his rights for Ben's benefit, but there is no trust.

For example, if Tom is the executor of a will under which Ben is the sole heir, Tom will be the legal owner of the deceased's assets before the will is executed and Ben will have a right that Tom transfer his title to those assets to Ben. However, Tom will not hold those assets on trust for Ben: *Commissioner of Stamp Duties (Queensland)* v *Livingston* [1965] AC 694. In Swadling's terms, holding rights as an executor is a different way of holding rights than holding rights as a trustee.

Again, Tom and Ben could enter into a contract where Ben undertakes to leave his house to Tom in his will, and Tom in return undertakes to keep the house sealed up for 10 years as a memorial to Ben. When Tom obtains the house under Ben's will, Ben's estate will have a contractual right – which will probably be specifically enforceable (*Beswick* v *Beswick* [1968] AC 58) – that Tom exercise his rights over the house so as to keep the house sealed up for 10 years in memory of Ben. But the courts do not recognise that it is possible to create a trust that has that effect: *Brown* v *Burdett* (1882) 21 Ch D 667. Again in Swadling's terms, the way in which a trustee holds rights does not permit those rights to be held subject to an obligation to deploy them in a way that the courts regard as 'useless' (*Brown*, at 673).

The better view seems to be that trusts law is (in this one respect only) akin to contract law. Contract law provides the most effective and reliable way of Tom's making a legally binding promise to Ben. But it is possible for Tom to make a legally binding promise to Ben without entering into a contract with Ben: *Hedley Byrne & Co Ltd* v *Heller & Partners* [1964] AC 465 (promise to take care binding under the law of negligence); *Central London Property Trust Ltd* v *High Trees House* [1947] KB 130 (promise not to sue binding under the law on estoppel); *R* v *North and*

East Devon HA, ex parte Coughlan [2001] QB 213 (promise not to close NHS facility binding under public law). In the same way, trusts law provides the most effective and reliable way of Tom's holding rights subject to an obligation to apply those rights on behalf of a person or purpose – but it is possible for Tom to come under such an obligation (particularly through entering into a contract with someone else) without a trust arising, as the examples in the last two paragraphs show.

John Langbein has argued that there exists a deeper connection between trusts law and contract law. In the case where Sal transfers assets to Tom to be held on trust for Ben (or, in lawyers' terminology, Sal 'settles' assets on Tom to be held on trust for Ben, with Sal being known as the 'settlor' and Ben the 'beneficiary' (or *cestui que trust*) of the trust that Sal seeks to set up), Langbein argues that the root of Tom's obligation to administer the trust assets on behalf of Ben is Tom's *promise* to Sal that he will do exactly that: Langbein 1995. If cases of a promise being legally binding without a contract being entered into are examples of (to borrow a phrase from Robert Stevens) 'contract lite' (Stevens 2008), then on Langbein's view, trusts law is 'contract supermax strength': an area of law that does far more than contract law normally would to ensure that Tom's promise to Sal to hold assets for Ben's benefit is not only legally binding but will be performed.

Langbein concedes that his 'contractarian' account of the basis of trusts law has greater difficulties handling the case where Sal declares that she holds assets on trust for Ben (Langbein 1995, 627–28, 672–75). However, he goes too far when he says that 'the declaration of trust cannot be squared with the contractarian account of the trust, which finds the basis of the trust obligation in the trustee's promise to the settlor to hold the trust assets for the benefit of the beneficiary' (at 672). If Sal declares that she holds assets on trust for Ben *but does not tell* Ben, the courts are likely to regard Sal's declaration as a 'sham', designed to defraud Sal's creditors (*Midland Bank Plc* v *Wyatt* [1997] 1 BCLC 242) – if the creditors come knocking, Sal will say that the assets that are in her name are unavailable to pay off her debts as they are held on trust; if they don't, Sal will conveniently forget all about the 'trust' that she purported to create for Ben's benefit and no one will be any the wiser. So in the case where Sal declares that she holds assets on trust for Ben and makes that declaration effective by telling Ben she has made it, it is possible to argue that the foundation of Sal's obligations to Ben is Sal's promise to Ben that she will apply the trust assets for Ben's benefit.

However, Langbein's contractarian account of the foundation of a trustee's obligations is very hard to reconcile with the fact that a trustee occupies an office; which office the law maintains by ensuring it is always filled ('a trust will not fail for want of a trustee') and which office the law helps the trustee discharge by exercising an 'advisory jurisdiction' under which the trustee who is doubtful as to what they should do can go to the court for advice as to where his duty lies (something which a contractor is not able to do): Clarry 2018. It seems that the trustee is bound not so much by their word, but by the responsibilities of the office they have agreed to occupy by becoming a trustee.

The better view of the basis of a trustee's obligations seems to be that when a trustee is bound to apply trust assets for the benefit of a particular person or purpose, the trustee is bound because the judges – at first, just a group of judges, but eventually all judges in all common law jurisdictions – took the view that it was desirable that people should be able (if they wished) to hold rights subject to an obligation to apply those rights for the benefit of a particular person or purpose. And they devised the trust as a means (the most reliable and effective means) of allowing rights to be held in this kind of way. But who were the judges who took this view, and why did they take it? Answering that question takes us into the next section of the chapter.

2. HISTORY

THE USE

Like a Hollywood actor, the trust began its life under a different name: *the use*. The use originally performed a religious function. Crusaders going to war in the 12th and 13th centuries would try to protect the interests of the family they left behind by conveying (or 'feoffing') their land to a trusted friend, so that the land was held 'to the use of' the crusader's wife and children. The friend would be called a 'feoffee to uses' and the wife and children would each be a 'cestui que use'. Monks who had taken a vow of poverty would not be able to accept the gift of land to build a monastery on: but the land could be given to a trusted third party and held 'to the use of' the monks. What happened if the feoffee to uses betrayed the trust that had been placed in them is not clear, but evidently the procedure for creating a use over land proved reliable enough that people became interested from the 14th century onwards in taking advantage of this procedure in order to circumvent the rule that land could not be disposed of in a will.

Before 1540 what happened to your land, Blackacre, after you died was determined by the law: Blackacre would pass to your eldest son. The rule was feudal in nature: the eldest son got Blackacre because he was most likely to be able to perform the military services owed to the lord from whom Blackacre was held. But the rule prejudiced the interests of wives, daughters, and younger sons. In order to protect their interests, from the 14th century onwards it became increasingly common for the owner of Blackacre to convey Blackacre to a number of trusted individuals 'to the use of' the members of his family. That way, when the owner died, nothing changed: Blackacre was still held by the feoffees, who held it to the use of the owner's family. And if one of the feoffees died, again nothing changed: Blackacre was still held by the remaining feoffees. This had the side effect of allowing everyone involved to avoid paying the taxes that would be due (to the king, or the lord from whom Blackacre was held) when the owner of Blackacre died and Blackacre passed to his eldest child under the feudal rule of primogeniture.

This last effect of allowing land to be conveyed 'to the use of' another doomed uses (under that name) in the long run, but not before the Court of Chancery had become seriously involved with upholding and enforcing uses. The English common law was administered by the King's courts but how they did that job was superintended by the King's Chancellor, who could be appealed to in cases where the common law seemed to be behaving in an unjust or *inequitable* manner. From about 1350 onwards, these petitions were heard instead by a new court – the Court of Chancery – and out of this court's decisions emerged a body of law known as *Equity*. Unaccountably, the common law courts did nothing to uphold arrangements where land was held 'to the use of' another despite the popularity of those arrangements: by 1500, most land in England was held 'to the use of' another (Swadling 1996, 113). So it fell to the Court of Chancery to pick up the slack and enforce uses. (Maitland estimates that the Court first intervened in this way at some point between 1396 and 1403: Maitland 1905, 87.) Ever since then both uses and their successor, the trust, were identified as owing their legal status to the law of Equity.

Despite the moralistic rhetoric around the interventions of the Court of Chancery, we need not ascribe any high-minded motive to the Court in enforcing uses. The judges of the Court were paid out of the fees they earned by hearing cases. No cases, no fees, no judges. Hearing cases involving uses was too good an opportunity to turn down for a new court looking for business. As Frederic William Maitland observed (using the word 'trust' rather than 'use'), 'I think it might be said that if the Court of Chancery saved the Trust, the Trust saved the Court of Chancery' (ibid, 84). Maitland went on to speculate (at 89) about the first time the Court of Chancery intervened to enforce a use: 'When we consider where the king's interest lay, it is somewhat surprising that the important step should be taken by his first minister, the Chancellor. It seems very possible, however, that the step was taken without any calculation of loss and gain. We may suppose a scandalous case. Certain persons have been guilty of a flagrant act of dishonesty, condemned by all decent people ... [The Chancellor] compelled the [feoffees to uses] to do what honesty required. Men often act first and think afterwards.'

Uses fell out of use, at least under that name, after they were (literally) executed by Henry VIII in 1536. Fed up with the loss of tax revenue resulting from land being conveyed 'to the use of' another, Henry VIII persuaded Parliament to pass the Statute of Uses which 'executed' uses by providing that land held 'to the use of' another would be regarded as owned by that other. The Statute helped to trigger the most serious rebellion against Henry VIII's rule in his time as monarch: the Pilgrimage of Grace, originating in the North of England in 1536. The revolt forced Henry VIII to enact the Statute of Wills 1540, which for the first time allowed land to be left in a will. It might have been thought that this would cause people no longer to be interested in conveying land 'to the use of' another, but the practice was now entrenched and could not be reversed. Instead, conveyancing lawyers focussed their attentions on ways of circumventing the Statute of Uses.

One device was to convey land 'to Cat to the use of Tom to the use of Ben': it was argued that the Statute only had the effect of executing the first use, so that the land was actually conveyed to Tom 'to the use of Ben'. The common law courts rejected this argument in *Tyrrel's Case* (1557) 2 Dyer 155a, but it was later accepted by the Court of Chancery. Secondly, it was argued that the Statute only applied to cases where the feoffee to uses had no *active* duties under the use. A term was needed to describe a use which involved active duties: *trust* was the term that was settled on. It was therefore argued that the Statute of Uses did not apply to the case where land was conveyed to Tom to be held *on trust* for Ben.

A combination of these two points resulted in its becoming standard until 1925 (when the Statute of Uses was repealed) to convey land 'to Cat to the use of Tom, to hold on trust for Ben' (Baker 2019, 310), effectively conveying the land to Tom to hold on trust for Ben.

DEVELOPMENT OF THE MODERN TRUST

With these innovations, the trust was up and running and has never looked back. Key highlights in the trust's development into a recognisably modern form were:

(1) Charitable Uses Act 1601: while the state of the law on charitable trusts before 1601 is obscure, the better view seems to be that before 1601 the Court of Chancery did enforce trusts for charitable purposes and the 1601 Act was intended to assist the Court in this by creating commissioners who could be charged by the Court to investigate a particular charity (Story 1920, 479; Jones 1969, 22–23). The list of charitable purposes set out in the Preamble to the Act was to be hugely influential in determining what sort of purposes would be regarded as charitable (*Special Commissioners of Income Tax* v *Pemsel* [1891] AC 531) until the definition of charitable purposes was overhauled by the Charities Act 2006 (now 2011).

(2) *Lady Foliamb's Case* (1651) Godb 165: provided one of the first examples of a trust that was imposed under the law (otherwise known as a 'constructive trust') as opposed to one that is deliberately created by an individual. The trust is known as a vendor-purchaser constructive trust, and arises out of the case where Tom enters into a specifically enforceable contract with Ben to convey property to Ben. Tom will hold that property on a constructive trust for Ben under the equitable maxim 'Equity treats as done what ought to be done.'

(3) *Keech* v *Sandford* (1726) Sel Cas T King 61: arguably established another example of a constructive trust (a trust over property acquired by someone in circumstances where the prospect of acquiring or retaining that property might result in their acting in a way that would be wrongful), but more importantly established that where Tom holds assets on trust for Ben, Tom will not be allowed to benefit from the decisions that Tom takes as to how he

manages those assets (in *Keech*'s case, the decision was to accept the landlord's refusal to renew a lease that the defendant held on trust for the claimant; having accepted the refusal, the defendant was not allowed to try to take the lease for himself).

(4) *Dyer* v *Dyer* (1788) 2 Cox Eq 92: it had long been established that if Ben made a gift of land to Tom, it would presumed that Ben intended that Tom should hold that land to Ben's use (St Germain 1761, 164 (Dialogue II, Chap 21)). *Dyer* v *Dyer* extended this presumption to the case where Ben provided the money for land (Blackacre) to be purchased in Tom's name: in such a case Tom would be presumed to hold Blackacre on trust for Ben. But *Dyer* also made it clear this presumption could be rebutted, and would be in the case where Tom was Ben's son. In such a case, the most natural inference is that Ben intended to make a gift of the purchase money to Tom, and if a trust were to be established, Ben would have to prove that this was not the case and that he intended Tom should hold Blackacre on trust for him. To do this, Ben would have to show evidence in writing of the trust under the Statute of Frauds 1677. (The equivalent modern-day provision is s 53(1)(b) of the Law of Property Act 1925, which provides that a court will not acknowledge a declaration of trust over land unless it is evidenced in writing.)

(5) *Morice* v *Bishop of Durham* (1804) 9 Ves Jr 399, (1805) 10 Ves Jr 522: established the 'beneficiary principle' under which a trust that was not charitable would not be valid unless it was for the benefit of ascertainable individuals. In doing so, *Morice* held that a trust to advance purposes that were not charitable in nature would be invalid. The question of whether English law would give effect to non-charitable purpose trusts (and if so, when) continued to be posed, however, and the history of the struggles around this question will be considered in the following chapter.

(6) *Saunders* v *Vautier* (1841) 4 Beav 115: established that if Tom holds assets on trust for Ben (and only Ben), then so long as Ben is not a child, Ben will have the power to require Tom to hand those assets over to him, so that Ben will become the beneficial owner of those assets. This is so even if the settlor of the trust positively intended that Ben should not have access to the trust assets until Ben was much older (as happened in *Saunders* itself). What came to be known as 'the rule in *Saunders* v *Vautier*' was not followed in the United States, where it was ruled that Ben would not be able to

claim the trust property if doing so was inconsistent with the intentions of the settlor who created the trust: *Claflin* v *Claflin*, 20 NE
455 (1899). The result is somewhat curious: traditional, hidebound
England prioritises the wishes of living beneficiaries over probably
dead settlors, while the brash, swashbuckling USA makes the oppo-
site choice of allowing the wealthy to dictate the terms on which
their descendants will be allowed to enjoy that wealth (see Getzler
2009a).

(7)   *Milroy* v *Lord* (1862) 4 De GF & J 264: established the 'no recharacterisation' rule under which if Sal intends to transfer assets to Ben,
or transfer assets to trustees who will hold on trust for Ben, but the
transfer fails to go through, the law will not attempt to give effect to
Sal's intentions by recharacterising Sal's actions as amounting to a
declaration that Sal holds the assets on trust for Ben himself: 'there
is no equity in this Court to perfect an imperfect gift … [so that if
the gift] is intended to take effect by transfer [of the property from
Sal to Ben], the Court will not hold the intended transfer to operate
as a declaration of trust' (at 274–75, per Turner LJ).

(8)   *Pilcher* v *Rawlins* (1872) Ch App 259: established that assets held on
trust will lose that status if legal title to them is acquired by a bona
fide purchaser without notice (actual or 'constructive') of the fact
that they have been sold to the purchaser in breach of the trustee's
obligations under the trust. If Tom holds assets on trust for Ben,
and those assets are disposed of in breach of trust those assets will
continue to be held on trust for Ben if title to them is acquired by
someone who is not a bona fide purchaser without notice, such as a
volunteer (Vic) who received those assets as a gift.

Does that make Vic a trustee? Not necessarily (see Liew and
Mitchell 2017, 143). The mere fact that Vic is the legal owner of trust
assets is not enough to establish that Vic is a trustee: *Westdeutsche
Landesbank* v *Islington LBC* [1996] AC 669, 705 (per Lord Browne-
Wilkinson). If we think of being a trustee as like occupying an
office, it would have to be shown that Vic either agreed to assume
that office, with all its responsibilities, or Vic had sufficient knowledge on their part of where the trust assets came from that it would
fair to treat them *as though they had agreed* to assume that office (in
which case Vic would be known as a *trustee de son tort*).

But even if Vic is not a trustee, Ben will still have a right under
Saunders v *Vautier* (p 11) to demand that Vic hand over the trust

assets – if Ben can get to Vic in time, before the assets have been dissipated or transferred to a bona fide purchaser without notice. The bona fide purchaser of a legal interest without notice is known as 'Equity's darling' – Equity does not regard itself as having any jurisdiction to act against them or impress any obligations on them, which is why when they purchase trust assets they take them free and clear of any trust.

(9) *Barnes* v *Addy* (1874) LR 9 Ch App 244: established that a third party to a trust who 'assist[s] with knowledge in a dishonest and fraudulent design on the part of the trustees' (at 251, per Lord Selborne LC) will be held accountable for the breach of trust committed by the trustees, along of course with those trustees. In so ruling, the Court of Appeal in Chancery built on the Chancery Court's earlier ruling in *Eaves* v *Hickson* (1861) 30 Beav 136 that a defendant who knowingly *induces* a trustee to commit a breach of trust will be held liable for that breach of trust. So there are ways of being held liable for a breach of trust without being a trustee, but neither of these ways establish that the beneficiary under the trust has any kind of 'interest' in the trust property. A third party to a trust is held liable for a breach of trust not because they have damaged any 'interest' of the beneficiary's through their meddling but because their meddling has made them an accessory to the trustee's breach of trust (Davies 2015, 93–95, 98, 104–08).

THE TRUST IN THE POST-FUSION ERA

The trust remained the exclusive province of the Court of Chancery until near the end of the 19th century, when the Judicature Act 1873 abolished the distinction between courts of common law and courts of equity, so that 'every court shall recognize every kind of right, and, as occasion arises, either deal with it itself or hand it over to some more convenient tribunal' (Meagher, Gummow and Lehane 1992, 45, quoting one of the authors of the 1873 Act).

This move was prompted by the fact that, having been once so desperate for business at its inception in 1350, by the 1800s the Court of Chancery had taken on far more work than it was capable of handling. This was in part because of the complexity of the Court's procedures (Lobban 2004, 391–94) but also because of the range of its jurisdiction, especially its involvement in hearing bankruptcy cases (Getzler 2004, 605–06). The result was that by the start of the 19th century, cases heard in the Court of Chancery were subject to huge delays and high fees. The Court became so notorious for its inefficiencies that they formed the basis of Charles Dickens' 1853 novel *Bleak House*. The novel is centred on a fictional wills case, *Jarndyce* v *Jarndyce*, which may have been based on an actual case that took 62 years for the Court of Chancery to resolve (*Thelluson* v *Woodford* (1817) 1 Ves Jr 440).

The effect of the so-called 'fusion' of law and equity brought about by the Judicature Act was that trusts law fell into the hands of judges who did not necessarily self-consciously identify themselves as 'equity lawyers' (though at first instance, trusts cases were reserved for a newly created 'Chancery Division of the High Court' that still exists to this day). But this did not result in any evisceration of traditional trusts law doctrines and remedies. If anything, the post-fusion judges were *plus royaliste que le roi* when it came to trusts law. Two examples can be given.

In *Walsh* v *Lonsdale* (1882) Ch D 9, Walsh and Lonsdale entered into an agreement under which Lonsdale agreed that he would rent a weaving shed to Walsh for seven years. In order to do this Lonsdale had to use a deed to lease the shed to Walsh. This Lonsdale failed to do, so that when Walsh took possession of the shed, Walsh was treated under the common law as renting the shed from Lonsdale on a year-to-year basis. Under that kind of lease, Lonsdale was not entitled to be paid rent in advance. However, Lonsdale did demand rent be paid in advance and when Walsh failed to pay, Lonsdale seized Walsh's goods. The Court of Appeal ruled that Lonsdale was entitled to do this. Lonsdale may not have been entitled to seize Walsh's goods under the common law, but in Equity Walsh and Lonsdale would be regarded as having entered into a seven-year lease ('Equity treats as done what ought to be done') and Equity's view of the matter would prevail over the common law's.

In *Boardman* v *Phipps* [1967] 2 AC 46, Boardman was the solicitor to a trust fund that held shares in a textile company, Lester & Harris, which was underperforming. Boardman proposed to the trustees that they use their shareholding to take over the company and improve its performance. The trustees turned this proposal down, with the result that Boardman suggested that he might take over the company himself and run it. Boardman proceeded to do just that, buying shares in the company himself. He made a success of turning the company's fortunes around, so that both Boardman's shares and the trust fund's shares went up in value. Demonstrating the truth of the maxim that no good deed goes unpunished, the beneficiaries of the trust fund then sued Boardman for the profit he had made. The House of Lords applied the principle set out in *Keech* v *Sandford* (above) to find Boardman liable (though they awarded him an allowance for the work he had done to improve the company's performance). The decision seems harsh, and was summed up by the doyens of Australian equity law as follows: '[*Boardman* made] a solicitor liable to account ... for a profit his client could not and did not wish to make. Of the five judges who sat on the appeal, only two, Lords Cohen and Upjohn, had come from the Chancery Division and they disagreed [with the result]' (Meagher, Gummow and Lehane 1992, 39).

However, there *was* a radical change in the trust in the post-fusion era; a change of 'historic importance' (Langbein 2004, 57). If you look at the cases mentioned in the previous section, almost all of them involved trusts being used in a domestic context, as an instrument for the holding of property by families.

For example, *Barnes* v *Addy* was a case about a trustee holding property on trust for two daughters, Susan and Ann, and their children. The trustee, Susan's husband, having fallen out with Ann's husband, no longer wished to hold anything on trust for Ann and her children and conveyed Ann's share of the trust assets to Ann's husband, to hold on trust for his wife and children. The trust that gave rise to the litigation in *Pilcher* v *Rawlins* was 'made by Jeremiah Pilcher, under which J.G. Pilcher, G. Pilcher, and W.H. Pilcher were to stand possessed of £8373 in trust for Jeremiah Pilcher during his life, and after his death for his children by a former marriage' ((1872) 7 Ch App 259, 260). *Milroy* v *Lord* was about an attempt by a well-off man living in New Orleans to create a trust for the benefit of his favourite niece, with the husband of the niece attempting to sue the purported trustee of the trust (the father-in-law of the settlor) for not performing his supposed duties as trustee. And so on.

This domestic aspect of the law of trusts is preserved by the Law of Property Act 1925, which provides that where Blackacre is conveyed into the names of Jim and Jan, they will jointly hold the title to Blackacre (s 1(6)) on trust for themselves (s 36(1)), with Jim and Jan's equitable rights being held either jointly or in common (s 36). But whether as a result of trusts being affected in a post-fusion era by the more mercantile instincts of common law judges, or simply because of wider developments in the world during the late 19th century and 20th century, trusts today no longer focus on performing the domestic role that they almost exclusively played before the fusion of law and equity.

Instead, trusts are now primarily, in John Langbein's phrase, an 'instrument of commerce' (Langbein 1997) with Langbein estimating (at 166) that 'well over 90% of the money held in trust in the United States is in commercial trusts as opposed to personal trusts.' And equitable rules and doctrines have abandoned their traditional focus on constraining the excesses of the market (for that role, see McBride 2017, ch 4, and Samet 2018). Instead, they now *enable* those excesses by shaping the law of trusts so that it can provide a variety of vehicles for players in the market to achieve their commercial goals (see, generally, Zhang 2022):

(1)   *Wealth management trust.* We can define a wealth management trust as existing where trustees hold trust assets on trust for beneficiaries with the object of investing those assets with the object of producing financial returns for those beneficiaries. At any one time, the trust assets of a wealth management trust will typically consist of a mixture of 'intangibles, shares, bonds, bank balances ... [and] land ... leas[ed] for a money rent' (Penner 2014, 582). However, these assets will be so regularly traded for other assets that it makes more sense to think of the real subject matter of a wealth management trust as being a *fund*, which is made up at any one time of assets that are designated by the rules of the trust as belonging to the fund. As Maitland put it, 'the "trust fund" can change its dress, but maintain its identity. Today it appears as a piece of land; tomorrow it may be some gold coins in a purse; then it will be a sum of Consols; then it will be shares in a Railway Company, and then Peruvian Bonds ... All along the "trust fund" retains its identity' (Maitland 1905, 95; see also Noyes 1936, 69–78; Rudden 1994).

(2)   *Unit trust.* A unit trust is a kind of wealth management trust. It is 'a collective investment scheme under which ... property is held on trust for the participants' in the unit trust (Financial Services and Markets Act 2000, s 237(1)). The participants in a unit trust are known as 'unitholders'. Participants generate and buy units by contributing funds to the trust, and how many units they have determines the scope of the benefits they obtain under the trust. So the size of a unit trust is open-ended: the more people who participate in it, the greater the funds available to the trust, the more units that will be held in the trust.

(3) *Pension fund.* A pension fund consists in assets that are usually held on trust for employees who contribute to the fund (along with their employer) in the expectation that the assets of the fund will be invested so as to provide contributing employees with financial benefits after they retire. (See, generally, Donald 2020.) A pension fund is slightly different from a wealth management trust in that what benefits the contributing employees can claim under the trust are limited by the terms of the pension, so that if the fund is invested so well and wisely that the fund is likely to be able to meet all claims that can be made on it and still have assets left over, these surplus assets cannot be claimed by the contributing employees for whom they are supposedly held on trust but will instead be shared out among the employees and their employer in proportion to their contributions to the pension fund: *Air Jamaica Ltd* v *Charlton* [1999] 1 WLR 1399. However, all such talk of surpluses is for the birds nowadays. Most pension funds struggle to meet the legitimate claims that are made on them, with the result that pension funds have started to resemble Ponzi schemes, which keep up the impression of being financially healthy by paying out to members of the scheme from contributions made by new recruits to the scheme.

(4) *Intermediated security.* An intermediated security is a security (a share or a bond) that is not straightforwardly held on trust by Tom for Ben. Instead, one or more intermediaries stand between Tom and Ben, so that Tom holds on trust for Cat, who holds on trust for Dan, who holds on trust for Eve, who holds on trust for Ben at the end of the chain. None of the intermediaries drop out (we observed earlier on p 3 that this was the case with sub-trusts), so Ben does not have any rights directly against Tom in respect of the security held by Tom, but instead only has rights against Eve, who only has rights against Dan, who only has rights against Cat, who only has rights against Tom. This is known as the 'no look through' principle for intermediated securities.

The advantage of this set-up is that it allows Ben to make investments in (for example) shares in Company X quickly, easily and relatively cheaply by dealing with Eve. The disadvantage is that under the 'no look through' principle, Ben's 'investment' gives Ben no ultimate rights in relation to how the shares in Company X are used in voting on, for example, the appointments and salaries of directors of Company X. The Law Commission has pondered whether the solution to this problem might be to take a leaf out of Henry VIII's book and 'execute' intermediated securities so that in the above set-up, Tom will hold on trust directly for Ben (Law Commission 2020, ch 8) – but it has ultimately opted against such a drastic solution.

(5)   *Client and customer trust.* Client and customer trusts take advantage of the 'asset-partitioning' effect of a trust to allow clients and customers to pay over money to a firm, safe in the knowledge that if they don't receive what they have paid for, they will be able to recover their money even if the firm is insolvent (which is probably why the client/customer has not received what they paid for). This will be because the money they paid over was held on trust for them unless and until they receive what they paid for.

All of these trusts serve a business purpose. The first four encourage ordinary people to invest their earnings, thus providing banks and businesses with the capital that they need to function and flourish. The last encourages ordinary people to extend credit to businesses – providing them with money in advance of receiving what that money is supposed to pay for – by reassuring them that they will not lose out by doing so. But in order for trusts like these to exist, ideas about trusts that were commonplace in the age when trusts performed a purely domestic function also had to be jettisoned.

First, the idea that 'Almost every well-to-do man [could be] a trustee' (Maitland 1905, 97). Fulfilling the office of a trustee nowadays requires expertise that is out of reach for ordinary people. Second, the idea that trustees should not profit from their position as trustee. That is now an 'inaccurate incantation' – the modern trustee 'is usually a professional [who] expects to be paid for his services' (Millett 1998, 216). Third, the idea that the powers of investment of a trustee should be strictly limited so as to safeguard the beneficiaries under the trust from the possibility that the trustee would exercise those powers improvidently. The commercial needs of banks and businesses for the supply of capital trumped this concern to protect beneficiaries, with the result that the strictly limited list of authorised investments laid out in s 1 of the Trustee Act 1925 was replaced 75 years later by a 'general power of investment' under s 3 of the Trustee Act 2000. This provides that unless the trust instrument says otherwise 'a trustee may make any kind of investment that he could make if he were absolutely entitled to the assets of the trust.'

The commercialisation of trusts law towards the end of the 19th century and over the course of the 20th century has therefore resulted in trusts becoming the exclusive playground of an elite cadre of professionals, who hold themselves out as skilled and knowledgeable in matters of high finance and expect to be well-paid for that skill and knowledge. The effects of this, it can now be judged, have been economically disastrous, as will be explained further in chapter five. But the true economic effects of trusts law can only be appreciated properly by grasping how far the concept of the trust has spread all over the globe.

3. THE INTERNATIONAL DIMENSION

The trust went wherever the British Empire went: there is no common law jurisdiction in the world that does not know what a trust is and give effect to it. Perhaps influenced by the (incorrect) ideas (a) that the trust rests on a schizophrenic recognition of two different people (the trustee and the beneficiary) as being 'owners' of the trust property at different levels of the legal system (which idea is rejected by Maitland 1936, 17–18); or (b) that a trust involves an unacceptable splitting of the incidents of what it means to own something, with the trustee retaining the rights of control over the trust assets, and the beneficiary obtaining the rights to benefit from the trust assets (see Honoré 1961, 142–43), civilian jurisdictions have been traditionally unwilling or unable to enable people to create trusts or trust-like arrangements. However, the flexibility and usefulness of the trust, particularly in commercial contexts, has caused that hostility to weaken and now jurisdictions like Quebec (Civil Code of Quebec, Art 1260f), the Czech Republic (Swadling 2016), Japan (Trust Act of Japan 2006), and China (Trust Law of the People's Republic of China 2001) enable people to create what are recognisably trusts.

Civilian countries like the Netherlands, Italy and Switzerland are signatories to the Hague Trusts Convention (from which one of our original definitions of a trust was taken). As a result, they are required to recognise and give effect to a trust created under the law of a jurisdiction that has signed up to the Convention, unless the 'significant elements' of the trust are closely associated with a jurisdiction that does not empower people to create trusts of that kind (Art 13). The UK is also a signatory to the Hague Trusts Convention, but in incorporating the Convention into domestic law via the Recognition of Trusts Act 1987, it did not provide for trusts not to be recognised on the grounds of Art 13. The result is that the English courts are seemingly bound to recognise and give effect to a trust created *in England* that English trusts law does *not* allow people to create, provided that the instrument creating the trust specifies that it will be governed by (say) the law of trusts in the Cayman Islands, and under *that* law people are enabled to create that kind of trust (Smith 2013, 94).

The fact that jurisdictions across the world enable people to create trusts has set off a vicious 'race to the bottom' among those jurisdictions. The race gets started as follows. A particular country or territory – call it Bleakistan – enjoys little by way of natural resources or other amenities that could underpin its economy and provide jobs for those who live there. (See, for example, the British Governor's description of the Cayman Islands as 'no tropical paradise ... [they have] a mosquito-ridden beach ... a pleasant but very untidy little town [and] swamp clearance schemes which generate smells strong enough to kill a horse': Shaxson 2012, 109.) To make up for this, Bleakistan gets into the business of offering financial services to wealthy people living elsewhere in the world ('*offshore*'), promising them that they can settle some of their wealth within Bleakistan on trusts that offer advantages that are not available within the jurisdiction where the wealthy person lives. As a result, wealth starts being transferred into Bleakistan, and Bleakistan's economy and people prosper. Desertia – a neighbouring country which has as few natural advantages as Bleakistan – sees how well Bleakistan is doing offering financial services to sources of offshore wealth, and decides to get into the same game. But to get anywhere in attracting offshore wealth to come to Desertia, it has to 'outbid' Bleakistan and offer people living elsewhere in the world even more generous terms on which they can settle their wealth on trust in Desertia. And if this works to attract wealth away from Bleakistan and towards Desertia, then Bleakistan will have to make an even more generous offer to settlors than Desertia, and so on, and so on.

While Bleakistan and Desertia duke it out in this way, a jurisdiction like Arcadia – which is blessed with lots of natural advantages and, as a result, a lot of local ('*onshore*') wealth – cannot be indifferent to what Bleakistan and Desertia are doing. This is because what they are doing is liable to result in a lot of wealth flowing out of Arcadia and into the part of the world where Bleakistan and Desertia are located. So Arcadia will also come under pressure to at least match the offer that jurisdictions like Bleakistan and Desertia are making to sources of wealth that count as offshore to Bleakistan and Desertia, but are onshore so far as Arcadia is concerned because that is where those sources of wealth reside. If Arcadia succumbs to that pressure (an example of this may be the UK's failing to incorporate Art 13 of the Hague Convention into its domestic law: Smith 2018, 2164), then it will end up joining Bleakistan and Desertia in dancing to an increasingly frenetic tune that reflects the ever-more rapacious demands of the super-wealthy who live in places like Arcadia.

Some of the innovations that this race to the bottom have produced are:

(1) *STAR trusts.* Under the Cayman Islands' Special Trusts (Alternative Regime) Law 1997, settlors are able to settle assets on a non-charitable purpose trust – known, because of the name of the Law under which it is created, as a 'STAR trust' – and appoint enforcers to ensure that the trust assets are applied for that purpose. At least one of the trustees of the trust must be a trust company that is licensed to operate in the Cayman Islands.

(2) *VISTA trusts.* A VISTA trust (so-called because it is created under The Virgin Islands Special Trusts Act 2003) allows shares in a family business created by the settlor (and registered in the British Virgin Islands) to be held on trust for whoever the settlor specifies (normally, for the purposes of succession planning, other members of the settlor's family). What makes a VISTA trust special – and attractive to settlors – is that the trustee of a VISTA is not allowed to use their shareholding in the family business to 'interfere in the management or conduct of any business of the company' (s 6(2)(a)). Decisions over how the family business will be run are therefore left entirely up to the business' board of directors, which will usually comprise the settlor and other family members. Moreover, while the trustee will have the power to sell the shares in the family business, unlike a normal trustee they are under no duty to sell, or consider selling, the shares to enhance the value of the trust fund (s 9(2)); moreover, they cannot sell the shares without the consent of the directors of the company.

(3) *Asset protection trusts.* Beginning with the Cook Islands in the South Pacific (see Barnett 2022, 368–71), an increasing number of trust jurisdictions (including numerous American states) enable settlors to create 'asset protection trusts' where they can settle property on trust for themselves but at the same time protect those trust assets from being accessed by their creditors (see, generally, Sterk 1999).

Under s 13A of the Cook Islands' International Trust Act 1984, a trust set up under its provisions will remain valid in the event of the settlor's bankruptcy even if the trust is for the benefit of the settlor or their family, and will 'take effect according to its tenor' unless a creditor of the settlor can establish under s 13B that the trust was created with the principal intent of defrauding that creditor and deprived the settlor of the means to pay off the creditor.

(4) *Reserved powers for settlors.* Traditionally, where Sal settles assets on Tom to hold on trust for Ben, Sal drops out of the picture and the future administration of the trust is simply a matter between Tom and Ben. However, settlors cannot be expected to be happy with this traditional position when they are transferring wealth halfway round the world to a country or territory of which they know very little. In order to provide them with the necessary reassurance that their wealth is safe and secure, many trust jurisdictions allow Sal to reserve to herself numerous powers to interfere with how the Tom-Ben trust operates, without the trust that Sal has purported to create either being declared a sham or the law's finding that Tom in fact holds the trust assets on trust for Sal and not Ben (see, generally, Ho 2018).

For example, Art 9A of the Trusts (Jersey) Law 1984 provides that if Sal's trust is created under Jersey law, Sal may reserve to herself powers '(a) to revoke, vary or amend the terms of [the] trust'; (b) to direct how the income or capital of the trust will be applied; (c) where the trusts consist in shares in a company, to give directions how the shares are to be used to engineer the appointment or removal of an officer of the company; (d) to direct how the trust assets are to be applied; (e) to appoint or remove any trustee or enforcer of the trust; (f) to appoint or remove any investment adviser to the trust; (g) to change the law that applies to the trust; (h) to require that the trustee's powers over the trust assets only be exercised with Sal's consent.

The result of these provisions is that Sal can settle assets on Tom to be held on trust for Ben and Tom will be effectively Sal's puppet – but Sal's creditors will still be prevented from making any claim on the assets that Sal has settled on Tom to hold on trust for Ben, as those assets will no longer count as Sal's.

(5) *Trusts over factual powers.* We have already seen that the subject matter of a trust will consist in rights that Tom holds either in

law or in equity. So a trust is a legal concept that is built on top of another legal concept (a right). It should therefore be impossible to find that Tom holds a factual power on trust for Ben. For example, Tom may have the factual power to walk from Lands' End to John O'Groats – but he cannot hold that power on trust for Ben so that he is duty-bound to exercise that power for Ben's benefit.

However, this limit on the concept of a trust has been breached as a result of the rise of cryptocurrencies and a desire on the part of a large number of jurisdictions to enable the factual powers Tom possesses over a certain quantity of (say) bitcoin in a wallet to be held on trust for Ben (see, generally, Low 2021). Of course, the formal proprieties are observed by declaring that bitcoin (or some other cryptoasset) amounts to property and can *therefore* be held on trust. However, it is clear that the true order of things is that a desire to enable people's factual powers over bitcoin to be held on trust is leading law-makers to declare that bitcoin amounts to property.

The result of these innovations has been to undermine the definitions of a trust considered at the start of this chapter, and dilute the concept of a trust so much that it is difficult to say now what a trust actually is (Alexander 2013; Hofri-Winogradow 2015). Some indication of how far we have come is provided by a recent attempt by Lusina Ho to define 'the essential elements of the trust relationship' (Ho 2013, 1).

She argues that the essential features of a trust are fourfold: (1) 'the trustee has powers to manage the property and to alienate the assets free from the beneficiary's rights'; (2) 'the trust assets and properties representing them from time to time are immune from the claims of the trustee's heirs, spouses and personal creditors'; (3) the beneficiary 'has the right to obtain trust assets subject to the terms of the trust and to make claims against third parties who receive trust properties upon an unauthorized disposition by the trustee'; and (4) 'there is a check and balance mechanism to ensure that the trustee uses [their] powers for the best interest of the beneficiary and not for his own benefit' (Ho 2013, 3–4).

However, so far as 'managing' the trust assets is concerned, (1) is not true of a *bare trust*, where Tom holds assets on trust for Ben and those assets are either to be transferred to Ben or someone nominated by Ben; neither are they true (as we have just seen) of VISTA trusts. And where a trustee like Tom does have the power to 'manage' the trust assets, while it may be part of the 'irreducible core' of a trust that he not spend those assets on himself, it is not necessarily the case (as we have seen under Art 9A of the Trusts (Jersey) Law 1984) that they will hold those assets subject to an obligation to apply them in the best interests of the beneficiary.

So when we are told that Tom holds assets on trust for Ben, the definition of a trust has now been so whittled down that the most we could confidently infer from what we have been told is that (1) Ben will be able to claim the trust assets unless the terms of the trust specify otherwise, and (2) no one else should be able to benefit from the trust assets unless they are authorised to do so under the terms of the trust. This is not very much, and if all trusts simply consisted of these two incidents, they would hardly be worth studying. However, as we will see in chapters two to four, there is much more, and much more of interest, that can be said of the kinds of trusts that make up the heartland of trusts law and which formed the basis of the definitions of a trust with which this chapter began. As has already been promised, chapter five will take us back to where this chapter has ended, and consider the damage done by the international race to the bottom in defining what a trust is and can be.

2

Persons and Purposes

1. THE DISTINCTION

DIFFERENTIATION

The difference between trusts for persons and trusts for purposes is nicely illustrated by two cases, decided just five years apart: *Re the Trusts of the Abbott Fund* [1900] 2 Ch 326 and *Re Andrew's Trust* [1905] 2 Ch 48.

In the *Abbott Fund* case, a trust fund that had been set up by one Dr Abbott, to look after his family after he died in 1844, was plundered by the trustees of the fund so that there was nothing left once the last remaining trustee died in 1889. A friend of the family, a Dr Fawcett, made an appeal for funds to support Abbott's two remaining daughters. About £248 was raised (the equivalent of £29,000 in today's money, allowing for inflation) but then Fawcett died. A further appeal for funds was made by a friend of Fawcett's and more money came in to assist Abbott's daughters. Then in 1899, both of the two daughters died. There was £366 left in the fund to help them, and the question the Chancery Division had to answer was – what should happen to the money?

The same question arose in *Re Andrew*. A bishop called Barclay died in 1881, leaving behind seven young children. Barclay's friends rallied together to raise some money to help pay for the children's education, and they managed to raise £900 between them. Later on the money was used to buy seven shares in a bank, and sizeable dividends on those shares, were paid from time to time to the trustees of the shares. By the time the children were all grown up, the trustees still held on trust the seven shares, and £460 from dividend payments. The children sued, arguing that they were entitled to the shares and cash. Barclay's friends argued that any rights that the children might have had in relation to the money raised for them disappeared once the children's education finished, and that it was the friends who were entitled to what was left of what had been raised to educate Barclay's children.

There were three possible analyses the courts could have adopted of either of these cases. For convenience, let's develop these analyses by considering the situation where Sal gave £10,000 to Tom for the purpose of assisting Ben to do x, it has now become impossible to assist Ben to do x, but Tom till holds £4,000 of the original £10,000:

(1)   Tom held the £10,000 on trust for Ben – a trust for persons. The stipulation as to how the money was to be used was neither here nor there: it was merely, in lawyers' language, *precatory* (a pious hope, not binding on Tom, that the money would be used to help Ben to do x). So the £4,000 left in Tom's hands is still held on trust for Ben (or, if Ben is dead, Ben's heirs), and so Ben (or Ben's heirs) is entitled to claim that £4,000 under *Saunders* v *Vautier*.

(2)   Tom held as much of the original £10,000 on trust for Ben as was needed to assist Ben to do x – a trust for persons. The stipulation that the money should actually be used to assist Ben to do x was merely precatory, so Ben at any point could have claimed as much of the £10,000 as was needed to assist Ben to do x; and having obtained that money, Ben could have done what he liked with it. But now that it is impossible for Ben to do x, none of the money left in Tom's hands is held on trust for Ben. Instead, it is held on trust for Sal. The trust for persons that initially existed between Tom and Ben is known as a *Re Sanderson* trust, as it was in *Re Sanderson's Trust* (1857) 3 Kay & J 497 that this analysis of the relationship between Tom and Ben was first developed. The trust that now exists between Tom and Sal is also a trust for persons and is known as a *resulting* trust. It's called 'resulting' because one of the meanings of 'resulting' used to be 'To recoil, to rebound, to spring back' and in return for Sal's transferring title to the £10,000 to Tom, something is coming back to Sal: a right that the £4,000 left in Tom's hands be handed over to Sal. (The Oxford English Dictionary says this meaning of 'resulting' is 'Obsolete'. Not among lawyers it isn't: we will come back to the topic of resulting trusts in the next chapter.)

(3)   Tom held the £10,000 on trust for the purpose of helping Ben do x – a purpose trust. Now that it is impossible to help Ben do x, that

purpose trust has failed, with the result that the remaining £4,000 in Tom's hands is now held on trust – a resulting trust – for Sal, in line with the general rule that if Sal transfers assets to Tom to be held on trust and they cannot be so held, then those assets will be held on trust – a resulting trust – for Sal instead.

In the *Abbott Fund* case, analysis (1) was rejected, as the court concluded that the money left in the Abbott Fund was held on resulting trust for those who had contributed to the fund. It is uncertain whether the court adopted analysis (2) or (3) in reaching that conclusion. As we will see, orthodoxy would dictate that they adopted analysis (2), and did *not* find that the Abbott Fund was held on a purpose trust.

In *Re Andrew*, analysis (1) was adopted, with the result that the court held the money left in the fund for the children's education should be divided among the children. The fact that the money was given for the education of the children merely supplied the 'motive' (53) for what was an absolute gift of the money to the children. The *Abbott Fund* case was regarded as irrelevant because it was 'absolutely different from the case now before the Court' (52), not least because in this case 'the children are still alive' (ibid). Of course, if analysis (1) were correct, it would make no difference whether the children were still alive or not – if they were dead, the money left in the fund for their education would be held on trust for their next of kin. The suggestion that it *did* make a difference creates the suspicion that analysis (1) was adopted in *Re Andrew* and rejected in the *Abbott Fund* case not because of an objective construction of the intent of the contributors to the funds in those cases, but because the courts took the view that adopting analysis (1) might do some good in *Re Andrew*, while it could not in the *Abbott Fund* case.

THE BENEFICIARY PRINCIPLE

Why was analysis (3) not clearly adopted in either of the above cases? The reason is that doing so would have offended against what is called the 'beneficiary principle'. The beneficiary principle is conventionally traced back to *Morice v Bishop of Durham* (1804) 9 Ves Jr 399. In that case Sir William Grant MR held (at 404–05) that 'There can be no trust, over the exercise of which this Court will not assume a control; for an uncontrollable power of disposition would be ownership, and

not trust ... Every ... trust [other than a charitable trust] must have a
definite object. There must be somebody, in whose favour the Court can
decree performance.'

So where Sal transfers assets to Tom to hold on trust for a purpose,
and that purpose is not charitable in nature, Tom cannot hold the assets
on trust for that purpose because there is no one who can sue Tom to
ensure that Tom is using the assets for the purpose for which they were
transferred to him by Sal. (Where the purpose is charitable in nature, so
that Tom holds the assets on a charitable trust, there is no problem as the
Attorney General, the Charity Commission and 'any person interested
in the charity' is vested with powers to ensure that the trust is properly
performed: Charities Act 2011, ss 114–15.)

It might be objected that this is a pretty weak objection to Tom's being
able to hold the assets transferred to him for a non-charitable purpose.
What if the purpose is such that certain people are interested in its being
performed – why can't those people be given the power to sue Tom if Tom
threatens to misapply the assets that have been entrusted to him? (Ralph)
Goff J asked exactly the same question in *Re Denley's Trust Deeds* [1969]
1 Ch 373 and went on to conclude (at 383) that the beneficiary principle
'is confined to [invalidating] purpose or object trusts which are abstract
or impersonal.' The door was opened to validating non-charitable
purpose trusts 'the carrying out of which would benefit an individual
or individuals, where that benefit is [not] so indirect or intangible ...
[that] those persons [could be given] locus standi to apply to the court
to enforce the trust'.

On that understanding of the beneficiary principle, analysis (3) *could*
have been adopted by the court deciding the *Abbott Fund* case. The court
could have held that so long as Abbott's daughters were alive, the monies in the Abbott Fund were held on a non-charitable purpose trust to
support them, with the daughters having standing to enforce that trust
if the trustees threatened to misbehave. However, as we will see, the
door opened in *Re Denley* to recognising non-charitable purpose trusts
as valid where the purpose of trust benefitted individuals who could be
given standing to enforce it was slammed shut almost as soon as it was
opened, in favour of a much stronger understanding of what the beneficiary principle entails.

That stronger understanding is represented by statements such as
Roxburgh J's in *Re Astor* [1952] 1 Ch 534, at 541: 'The typical case of
a [non-charitable] trust is one in which the legal owner of property is

constrained by a court of equity so as to deal with it as to give effect to the equitable rights of another'; Harman J's in *Re Shaw* [1957] 1 WLR 729, at 744: 'one cannot have a trust, other than a charitable trust, for the benefit, not of individuals, but of objects'; Viscount Simonds' in *Leahy* v *Attorney-General of New South Wales* [1959] AC 457, at 479: 'a trust may be created for the benefit of persons as cestuis que trust but not for a purpose or object unless the purpose or object be charitable'; and Lord Evershed MR's in *Re Endacott* [1960] 1 Ch 232, at 246: 'No principle perhaps has greater sanction or authority behind it than the general proposition that a trust by English law, not being a charitable trust, in order to be effective, must have ascertained or ascertainable beneficiaries.'

On this view, the beneficiary principle states baldly that the only way of holding property on a purpose trust is if the purpose of the trust is charitable; trusts which are not charitable in nature must be, if they are to be valid, trusts for persons, not purposes.

POWERS

I have a power in relation to you if I have the ability to alter your position: the power is a factual power if I am able to alter your factual position; the power is a legal power if I am able to alter your legal position. So suppose Sal settles assets on Tom to hold on trust for Ben with the power to give some, all, or none of the income generated by those assets to Cat, with any income not given to Cat being held on trust for Ben. In this case, Tom has a legal power in relation to Ben and Cat: Tom's decisions as to whether to give any income from the trust to Cat, and if so how much, will affect both Ben and Cat's legal position.

Tom's power will be a *bare* power if Tom's only duty is to act honestly in exercising the power. (An example of Tom's acting dishonestly in exercising the power would be Tom's exercising the power in Dan's favour in return for Dan's agreeing to split equally with Tom any income that Tom transfers to Dan.) Tom's status as a trustee makes it unlikely that Tom's power will be regarded as a bare power: instead, it will be regarded as a *fiduciary* power, with the result that Tom will not only have a duty to act honestly in exercising the power but a duty to consider exercising the power from time to time.

The reason for introducing all these definitions is that while the idea of a trust for a purpose is problematic, there is no problem with the idea of a power for a purpose. Indeed, a power without a purpose would be void because it would be 'capricious' (*In Re Manisty's Settlement* [1974] 1 Ch 17, 27). The inability to know *why* the power had been created would 'negative[] a sensible consideration by the [power holder] of the exercise of the power' (ibid, per Templeman J). In the case where Sal transfers assets to Tom to hold on trust for Ben, with the power to apply those assets or the income derived from those assets for a non-charitable purpose *x*, such a set-up will not offend against the beneficiary principle because the assets held by Tom, and the income derived from those assets, will be held on trust for Ben unless and until they are applied for purpose *x*. So the only trust that exists here is a trust for persons (as demanded by the strong form of the beneficiary principle); and the existence of that trust effectively prevents Tom misapplying the assets and income in his hands (as demanded by the weaker form of the beneficiary principle) because if Tom attempts to do this, Ben will be able to sue Tom.

For example, in *Re Shaw* [1957] 1 WLR 729, the author George Bernard Shaw left money in his will to be used for the purpose of creating a new British alphabet, comprising 40 letters rather than 26. It was held that the provision was invalid: a trust for such a purpose would not be charitable and there could be no such thing as a trust for a non-charitable purpose. Harman J held, however, that had Shaw provided that the money would be held on trust for his next of kin subject to a power for some or all of the money to be used for creating a new British alphabet, that would have been perfectly valid – though it would have gone only part of the way to realising Shaw's intentions as the power holder could not have been compelled to use the money to create a new British alphabet, and had the power holder chosen 'to pay the whole moneys to the [next of kin], no one [could] complain' (746). Half a loaf is better than none, though, and Shaw would have been doubtless happy had the purpose trust in his will been reconstrued as a power for a purpose and validated to that extent. However, Harman J held that 'I am not at liberty to validate this trust by treating it as a power' (ibid). The same stance was taken by Lord Evershed MR in *Re Endacott* [1960] 1 Ch 232, at 246: 'the proposition ... that if these trusts should fail as trusts they may survive as powers, is not one which I think can be treated as accepted in English law.'

This proposition may not have been accepted in English law, but it is accepted elsewhere. In Ontario, s 16(1) of the Perpetuities Act 1990 provides that 'A trust for a specific non-charitable purpose that creates no enforceable equitable interest in a specific person shall be construed as a power to appoint the income or the capital' unless there is some further reason – above and beyond the fact that the trust is for a non-charitable purpose – for regarding the trust as invalid (for example, that it is a trust 'for an illegal purpose or a purpose contrary to public policy'). And as we will see, even in English law, if Sal transfers assets to Tom to hold those assets on a non-charitable, and therefore invalid, purpose trust, the result will be that Tom will hold those assets on a resulting trust for Sal subject to a power to apply the assets for the purpose for which he was given them.

2. TYPES OF TRUSTS FOR PERSONS

We have already come across a number of different trusts for persons: (1) a bare trust, where Tom holds assets on trust for Ben, subject to an obligation to dispose of those assets as Ben directs; (2) a wealth management trust, where Tom holds a fund on trust for Ben, subject to an obligation to invest the fund with a view to growing the capital of the fund and generating income for Ben; (3) a resulting trust, where Tom derives assets from Sal and holds those assets on trust for Sal. Other examples of trusts for persons are:

FIXED TRUSTS

Under a fixed trust, the interests of the beneficiaries under the trust are fixed by the terms of the trust. This would be the case, for example, if Tom held assets on trust for Ben, Cat, Dan and Eve in equal shares. The interests of the beneficiaries under a fixed trust may be *conditional*. Ben's rights under a trust will be subject to a *condition precedent* if Ben only *acquires* a right under the trust if a certain condition is satisfied. An example is if Tom holds assets on trust for Cat, with an obligation to pay the income from those assets each year to that year's winner of the London Marathon, and Ben happens to be this year's winner. Ben's rights under the trust will be subject to a condition *subsequent* if Ben *ceases* to have rights in respect of the trust assets if a certain condition is satisfied.

An example would be if Tom holds a fund on trust for Ben, with the income from that fund being paid to Ben every year, but if Ben gets married, Tom will then hold the fund on trust for Cat.

Where the condition on someone's having an interest under a trust seems tainted by an illegitimate purpose, the courts may strike that condition down on the grounds of its being contrary to public policy. For example, a provision in a will that says, '1,000 shares in X Plc to be held on trust for my daughter, and the income from the shares applied for her benefit, until she gets married, at which point the shares are to be distributed in equal shares to my surviving brothers' seems like a sensible way of providing for one's daughter until she is firmly established in a new life. But a provision in a will that says, '1,000 shares in X Plc to be held on trust for my wife, and the income from the shares applied for her benefit, unless and until she remarries, at which point the shares are to be distributed in equal shares to my surviving brothers' possibly takes on a more sinister aspect – as an attempt to exercise control over one's widow from beyond the grave and disincentivise her from moving on with her life.

In *Re Lovell* [1920] 1 Ch 122, the testator's will bequeathed an annuity of £750 (about £25,000 a year in today's money) to the woman he was living with when he died, provided that 'she shall not return to live with her husband … [or] remarry and subject to her leading a clean and moral life'. The court chose to construe this provision as more like our first example – an attempt to provide for his lover after he was gone until she could start a new life – and upheld it, rather than striking it down as akin to our second example – an attempt from beyond the grave to control how his lover lived her life. By contrast, in *Re Caborne* [1943] 1 Ch 224, a mother left all of her property to be held on trust for her son, where he would only get a life interest in her property so long as the son's wife was alive or he remained married to her – but if the son's wife died while the son was still alive or he divorced her, the son would become absolutely entitled to all her property. Simonds J held that this condition on the son's obtaining full title to his mother's property was invalid as contrary to public policy – it amounted to an attempt to meddle in, and undermine, the son's marriage. The condition was therefore struck down and it was held that the son was entitled to all of his mother's property. The people who would have inherited the mother's property had the son died still married to his wife got nothing.

DISCRETIONARY TRUSTS

Unlike a fixed trust, under a discretionary trust the interests of the beneficiaries under the trust are not fixed – the trustees of the trust have a power to decide how much the various beneficiaries will receive under the trust. This power is neither a bare power nor a fiduciary power because the duty of the trustees is not just to act honestly if they exercise the power, or to consider whether or not to exercise it from time to time – they are duty-bound to exercise their power to decide how much the beneficiaries will receive under the trust. For this reason, discretionary trusts are sometimes known as 'trust powers'. Because, as was observed above, you cannot have a power without a purpose, discretionary trusts are – in some respects – much more akin to purpose trusts than trusts for persons.

First, a discretionary trust will be struck down as invalid if there is no discernible purpose behind its creation that could guide the trustees in their deliberations as to who should get what under it, so that any decision the trustees did make would be doomed to be 'capricious'.

Second, in the case of a discretionary trust for an extremely wide class of people such as 'everyone in the world except for the settlor and the settlor's family' – supplemented with a letter of wishes to the trustees to avoid the trust's being capricious – it is very hard to say that the trust assets are held on trust for anyone. The better analysis is that they are held subject to an obligation to apply the assets in accordance with the settlor's wishes, with potential donees having standing to enforce the trustee's obligation (*Gartside* v *Inland Revenue Commissioners* [1968] AC 553, 617–18 (per Lord Wilberforce)).

Third, while *Re Smith* [1928] Ch 915 says that the potential donees under a discretionary trust have the power under *Saunders* v *Vautier* to join together and demand the trust assets, it is unrealistic to think that any such power could be exercised where the discretionary trust is for an extremely large class of people, just as there can be no power under *Saunders* v *Vautier* to collapse a purpose trust.

Fourth, just as a purpose trust can be given some effect by recharacterising it as a fixed trust subject to a power to apply the trust assets for a particular purpose, Lionel Smith observes that the modern preference is not to create the classic types of discretionary trusts described above – he claims 'such structures are rarely created' (Smith 2017, 24) – but to vest

assets in a trustee to be held on trust for a charity, with a fiduciary power
to divert the assets or the income therefrom to any one of a very large
class of beneficiaries. In practice, the charity will never see any of the
assets that are nominally held on trust for it and exists purely to ensure
that this set-up satisfies the beneficiary principle (see, further, p 112). It is
this set-up that Smith refers to as a 'massively discretionary trust'.

It is possible to combine fixed trusts with discretionary trusts to
achieve interesting effects. For example, under a *protective* trust (see
Penner 2022, 57–58) Tom will hold assets on trust for life for Ben, subject
to a provision that brings that fixed trust to an end should Ben go bankrupt, in which case the fixed trust for Ben is replaced by a discretionary
trust under which Tom will have the power to distribute the trust assets
or the income therefrom to a range of beneficiaries, including Ben. Ben's
creditors will not be allowed access to the assets held on trust by Tom in
the event of Ben's going bankrupt because Ben will have no right to the
assets under the discretionary trust that came into existence when Ben
went bankrupt. Ben will merely have a right that Tom consider whether
or not to distribute any trust assets or income to Ben – which Tom will
not, until Ben is discharged from bankruptcy. If Ben tried to set up a protective trust in order to shield his assets from his creditors, that would be
struck down as contrary to public policy (*Re Brewer's Settlement* [1896]
2 Ch 503, 506), but if Sal set up the trust for the benefit of Ben, desiring
that only Ben should benefit from her largesse and not B's creditors, that
is regarded as unobjectionable (even though Ben's creditors might have
been induced to lend to Ben as a result of the appearance of wealth that
Ben was able to project by virtue of the Tom-Ben fixed trust).

CONSTRUCTIVE TRUSTS

We will talk in detail about constructive trusts in the next chapter, but
for now it should be noted that constructive trusts are a type of trust
for persons. Where Tom holds assets on trust for Ben, that trust will be
constructive in nature if (1) the trust did not arise in response to someone's intending to create it, and (2) Tom did not derive the trust assets
from Ben. (1) reflects the essential feature of a constructive trust – that
it is imposed by law rather than responding to someone's exercising the
facility that the law provides to create a trust. (2) is necessary for the
time being to create a temporary partition in the reader's mind between

constructive and resulting trusts. The question of the relationship between resulting and constructive trusts will be considered much more fully in the next chapter.

3. CHARITABLE TRUSTS

The major category of purpose trust that will be valid is a charitable trust. In this section, we will discuss the requirements that have to be satisfied for a charitable trust to be created. We begin with a fundamental question over the meaning of the word 'charity' in the legal context.

THE MEANING OF CHARITY

One way of approaching this question would be to consider the criticism levelled at me and another academic lawyer that we were 'uncharitable' in preparing our respective reviews of another academic's book (Beever 2017). The criticism was that we had not made enough of an effort to understand what the academic was trying to say, or when criticising something he had said, had not thought enough about what they might say in response to those criticisms. Our lack of charity in reviewing the academic's book therefore involved a failure to do enough to put ourselves in their shoes.

So on this view, charity involves making the effort to see things through someone else's eyes, and respond accordingly. In other words, the virtue of charity enables one – in the philosopher G.A. Cohen's wonderful phrase – to find 'oneself in the other' (Cohen 2013, 143) and as a result respond to that other with compassion. On this view of the meaning of charity, charitable works would consist in the kind of things listed in the following Bible verses: 'I was hungry and you gave me something to eat, I was thirsty and you gave me something to drink, I was a stranger and you invited me in, I needed clothes and you clothed me, I was sick and you looked after me, I was in prison and you came to visit me' (Matthew 25:35–36).

Charity law firmly turned its back on this meaning of the word 'charity' in the case of *Special Commissioners of Income Tax* v *Pemsel* [1891] AC 531. Properties were settled on trustees subject to an obligation to apply the rents from those properties for the purpose of enabling missionaries belonging to the Protestant Episcopal Church to evangelise non-Christian nations. The question was whether this amounted to a charitable purpose, in which case the rents would be exempt from income tax. The case reached the House of Lords. Of the six judges who heard the case, two (Lord Halsbury LC and Lord Bramwell) held that evangelising non-Christian nations did not amount to a charitable purpose, taking a view of the meaning of charity very similar to that advanced above. Lord Bramwell argued (at 564) that 'a charitable purpose is where assistance is given to the bringing up, feeding, clothing, lodging, and education of those who from poverty, or comparative poverty, stand in need of such assistance'.

The majority in *Pemsel* identified a charitable purpose with – to borrow a phrase from John Gardner (Gardner 2000, 15) – 'public-spiritedness', where a public-spirited person is distinctively concerned with 'the provision and maintenance of public goods, such as sensitive policing, public education, a vibrant artistic culture, fine cityscapes, good government'. As a result, she is not motivated to deal with 'human deprivation *as such*' but only gets involved in tackling human deprivation because of 'the broader social advance that comes of dealing with that deprivation. Her spirit is that of earnest concern rather than that of spontaneous fellow-feeling: she cares about *the problem of poverty*, say, more than about *the plight of the poor*' and she responds to that problem/plight with *philanthropy*, rather than compassion (all quotes, ibid, 17; emphases in original).

The majority endorsed the approach of the Chancery Court to defining what is a charitable purpose, which was to refer to the Preamble to the Charitable Uses Act 1601 (mentioned in the previous chapter) so that anything that fell within the 'spirit and intendment' of the Preamble would count as a charitable purpose (see, for example, *Morice v Bishop of Durham* (1804) 9 Ves Jr 399, 405). Lord Macnaghten enumerated (at 583) what sort of purposes would fall within the 'spirit and intendment' of the Preamble: 'trusts for the relief of poverty; trusts for the advancement of education; trusts for the advancement of religion; and trusts for other purposes beneficial to the community, not falling under any of the preceding heads.'

What came to be known as the 'fourth head' of charitable purposes was a residual category, not covering literally any purpose that was beneficial to the community, but the kind of purposes that fell within the spirit and intendment of the Preamble but did not fall under the first three heads (such as helping the old and the sick, prisoners, and providing public amenities). But the reference to 'other purposes beneficial to the community' as summing up what sort of things would fall under the fourth head was revealing, showing that the majority's view of what counted as a charitable purpose was strongly influenced by the idea that charitable purposes were to be identified with the provision of public goods. And, indeed, it would be later made clear that – trusts for the relief of poverty aside – a trust for a charitable purpose would still not count as charitable if it was not 'public – ... for the benefit of the community or of an appreciably important class of the community' (*Verge* v *Somerville* [1924] AC 496, 499 (per Lord Wrenbury)). So, for example, a gift of money to assist the work of an order of cloistered nuns was held not to be charitable because it was impossible to identify any public benefit that would result from the gift being made, as the nuns – being cloistered – never mixed with the wider community: *Gilmour* v *Coats* [1949] AC 426. And a trust to bring about an end to medical experiments on animals was held not to be charitable because the question of whether it would be for the public benefit to bring such experiments to an end was a 'political' one on which the courts could not pronounce: *National Anti-Vivisection Society* v *Attorney-General* [1948] AC 31 (citing *Bowman* v *Secular Society* [1917] AC 406, 442 (per Lord Parker)).

It is arguable that the turn away from seeing charity as centred on the compassionate relief of suffering and towards seeing charity as involving the philanthropic promotion of public goods has been extremely damaging for the law of charity, for a number of different reasons:

First, the courts' agnosticism on 'political' questions in cases like *National Anti-Vivisection Society* is ironic given that the issue of what counts as a public good is inherently political. So the state of the law on charity post-*Pemsel* has meant that the courts have not been able to avoid considering inherently political questions when they have tried to determine (a) what counts as a charitable purpose and (b) when a trust that serves an admittedly charitable purpose can be said to be for the 'public benefit'. As Jeffrey Hackney observes, the courts are not equipped to do this: they do not have 'the sort of research departments needed to make empirical (as opposed to cultural) findings of "public benefit", and while the adversarial system may suit the resolution of disputes between parties, it is not well suited to what [is] in effect ... social and fiscal engineering' (Hackney 1987, 67). The result is that when judges do sally forth and pronounce on these issues, they regularly embarrass themselves and reveal political prejudices that it would be better for judges not to bring into the courtroom (see Hackney 1981, 119–23).

Second, there is, of course, another institution which is charged with providing public goods, which is the government (central and local). Having charity law focus on the provision of such goods has inevitably raised questions on all sides of the political spectrum about the relationship between charities and the government (see Harding 2020). On the right it is argued that charities should play a much larger role in providing public goods and take some of the pressure off government bodies and government spending to provide those goods instead. On the left it is argued that the existence of charities provides a crutch for the government when it comes to the provision of public goods, and that abolishing the charitable sector would force the government to do a much better job that it currently does of providing such goods. The left could also argue that the more the government becomes dependent on charities to perform its basic functions, the more power the people running those charities acquire over government and they acquire that power without any form of democratic accountability. As a result, the law on charity has become a political football between left and right, with the inevitable result that any integrity that that area of law might possess becomes very difficult to preserve as each side get their chances to remould charity law in their preferred image.

Third, compassion is rare, while philanthropic impulses are extremely common – particularly when indulging those impulses also serves one's self-interest. Thanks to the tax breaks provided to trusts and institutions that qualify for charitable status, a good living can be made out of running and working for charities, and a desire to enjoy such tax breaks can lead actors to push for charitable status for projects that it was already in their self-interest to pursue. As a result, the charitable sector needs to be constantly policed both by the Charity Commission and the courts to ensure that it does not become an instrument to promote the self-interest of individuals and businesses. Such policing is inevitably patchy, with the result that scandals that bring the charitable sector into disrepute are not uncommon. In the case of the courts, their policing role leads them to adopt some rules and doctrines that – as we will see – are at first sight puzzling and lead people to question the coherence of charity law.

These problems could have been avoided had charity law focussed, as Halsbury and Bramwell wanted it to do in *Pemsel*, simply on the compassionate relief of suffering. The charitable sector would have been much smaller, of less political interest, and much less liable to be abused. But we are where we are, and where we are will be briefly summarised below.

CHARITABLE PURPOSE

Some of the political heat and interest was taken out of the question of what sort of purposes count as charitable in nature as a result of the Charities Act 2006 (now 2011), which put the law on this question on a statutory footing.

More than a dozen purposes are now explicitly named as charitable in nature. The original three heads of charitable purposes (the relief of poverty, the advancement of religion, and the advancement of education) are retained under s 3(1) of the Act; as are other purposes that traditionally fell under the fourth head – the advancement of health or the saving of lives, the advancement of animal welfare, the advancement of environmental protection or improvement, and the promotion of the efficiency of the armed services or the emergency services. Section 5 of the Act confirms as charitable a purpose that was originally recognised as such under the Recreational Charities Act 1958 (because it did not fall comfortably within the 'spirit and intendment of the Preamble) – which is the provision of recreational facilities designed to improve the conditions of life of those who are intended to use it, and are open to everyone or to all men or all women or to a more limited class that needs them by reason of their youth, age, infirmity or disability, poverty or economic circumstances. Section 3(1) adds some new purposes as being charitable in nature that were either not recognised as charitable under the old four heads of charitable purposes, or only arguably so: the advancement of citizenship or community development; the advancement of the arts, culture, heritage or science; the advancement of amateur sport; and the advancement of human rights, conflict resolution or reconciliation, or the promotion of religious or racial harmony or equality or diversity. For good measure s 3(1) also provides that the relief of those in need because of youth, age, ill-health, disability, financial hardship or other disadvantage is a charitable purpose.

Despite this reform, the law on what amounts to a charitable purpose still has the potential to embroil the courts in difficult issues. It is established that a trust for the putting on of an exhibition cannot be said to be for the advancement of education if what is being exhibited is of no artistic or aesthetic merit (*Re Pinion* [1965] 1 Ch 85). Similarly, what can be said to be for the advancement of the arts may involve the courts' making a judgment about the value of the art being advanced (*Re Delius* [1957] Ch 299). It is unclear whether a similar scientific judgment has to be made about the efficacy of a therapy, such as faith healing, for a trust promoting that therapy to qualify as being for the advancement of health. The provision in s 3(2) of the 2011 Act that the concept of a religion includes 'a religion which involves belief in more than one god' and 'a religion which does not involve belief in a god' could not do more to pass the buck to the courts to decide what amounts to a religion and what does not, when it comes to deciding whether a particular trust can be said to be for the advancement of religion. More buck-passing underlies s 3(1)(m) of the 2011 Act, which confirms that any purpose recognised by the courts as charitable in the past and not mentioned in the Act is still charitable in nature, while also allowing the courts to recognise new categories of charitable purpose on the basis that they are analogous to purposes that have already been recognised as charitable.

PUBLIC BENEFIT

The requirement that a purpose trust, to qualify as charitable, must not only be for a charitable purpose, but for the public benefit as well has involved the courts in the most difficulties. A question that might have turned on a straightforward question of fact – would fulfilment of this purpose benefit an appreciable number of people? – now turns on the application of a number of rules of law, which seem to bear little relation to this straightforward question. However, this should not surprise us. If the courts have only two requirements to play with in deciding whether a purpose trust should count as charitable in nature – charitable purpose, and public benefit – it is only natural that one or both of those requirements will be distorted if the courts think that the gift of charitable status should be conditional on other, unstated, requirements being satisfied. That is what has happened to the public benefit requirement.

(1) *Personal nexus.* The House of Lords ruled in *Oppenheim v Tobacco Securities Trust Ltd* [1951] AC 297 that a trust for the education of children could not be said to be for the public benefit if all the children were ultimately linked to a common employer, so that there existed a

'personal nexus' between them, via their parents, and a single employer. Lord MacDermott dissented, reasonably enough, on the basis that the trust in *Oppenheim* had the potential to benefit more than 100,000 children (at 314).

21 years later, the reasoning in *Oppenheim* was criticised in *Dingle* v *Turner* [1972] AC 601, with Lord Cross endorsing Lord MacDermott's view that distinguishing between 'personal and impersonal relationships' as a basis for determining public benefit was not 'very satisfactory' (623), particularly when it came to trusts for the employees (or children of the employees) of very large employers (624). But Lord Cross still endorsed the result in *Oppenheim* on the basis of its 'practical merits' and a 'far broader' approach to the issue of public benefit (623). The practical merit of the decision in *Oppenheim* was that it denied charitable status – and consequent tax breaks – to a company's scheme to pay for its employees' children to be educated, a perk which could be very useful for both attracting good employees to join the company and deterring good employees from either leaving the company or allowing their performances to slip, thus endangering their continued employment at the company. Lord Cross thought that were such a scheme to be declared charitable, it would enjoy 'an undeserved fiscal immunity' (625) – undeserved because however meritorious the scheme might be, 'there is no reason why [the company's] fellow taxpayers should contribute to a scheme which by providing "fringe benefits" for ... employees will benefit the company by making their conditions of employment more attractive.'

The lesson is that a scheme should be denied charitable status on the ground of 'no public benefit' no matter how beneficial it might be to the public if the scheme is motivated by the self-interest of the person or company setting it up. There is no need to encourage through charitable status that which will be called forth by the 'invisible hand' of the market in any case.

(2) *Fees.* This is the reason why a profit-making entity cannot get charitable status, no matter how beneficial to the public its activities might be. But what about a non-profit-making entity that still charges fees for its services, ploughing everything it earns back into the running of the service? Can it be said not to be for the public benefit because one section of the community – the poor – will effectively not be able to benefit from the entity's services because its fees will be beyond their means?

In *Re Resch's Will Trusts* [1969] AC 514 (a fee-charging hospital) and *Joseph Rowntree Memorial Trust Housing Association* v *Attorney-General* [1983] Ch 159 (a housing association selling homes to retirees on a no-profit basis), charitable status was granted on the basis of indirect benefits to the community from having a fee-charging hospital in its presence in terms of taking pressure off state health resources (in *Re Resch*) and on the basis of the homes being available to a significant class of people who needed them (in *Rowntree*). These seem pretty orthodox bases for finding public benefit, though the application of those ideas to fee-charging institutions might be controversial (Hackney 1987). However, when the issue was revisited – in the context of fee-charging schools – in *R (Independent Schools Council)* v *Charity Commission* [2012] Ch 214, it was held that a fee-charging school could only argue that it existed for the public benefit if it went beyond making *de minimis* or token attempts to allow students from poor backgrounds to attend the school and made suitable provision for such students given the nature of the school ([215]–[217]).

If we were *just* concerned with whether a fee-charging school is for the public benefit, whether the school is accessible by all socio-economic classes would seem an odd criterion to focus on: a trust for the provision of educational scholarships for people from a deprived background would not be regarded as not for the public benefit just because the scholarships were only available to students from a particular socio-economic back-ground. However, on a 'far broader' approach to the issue of public ben-efit, we might argue that a trust should not enjoy charitable status – and consequent tax breaks funded by the general taxpayer – unless it operates in a way that is consistent with basic democratic values (see Chan 2016, 77–78). This would disqualify a trust that entrenches privilege (such as a trust for university scholarships for students from Eton) but not a trust that helps eliminate privilege (such as the aforementioned trust for edu-cational scholarships for students from underprivileged backgrounds). Whether a fee-charging school can really be said to be operating in a way that is consistent with basic democratic values is doubtful, but that seems to be what the *ISC* case was getting at in requiring such schools to make more than *de minimis* or token efforts to allow students from under-privileged backgrounds to benefit from what they have to offer.

(3) *Class within a class.* It has long been established that a purpose trust that only benefits a 'class within a class' cannot be said to be for the public

benefit and is therefore not charitable. This limit was applied in *Inland Revenue Commissioners* v *Baddeley* [1955] AC 572 to find that the gift of land for the purpose of educating and providing recreational facilities for Methodists and people thinking of becoming Methodists who lived in West Ham and Leyton was not charitable. Lord Reid dissented in *Baddeley* on the basis that these limitations on who could benefit from the gift of land did not prevent those could benefit amounting to 'an appreciably important class of the community' (606). But Lord Simonds' judgment reveals the real reason for the 'class within a class' limit on the courts' willingness to find that a purpose trust is for the public benefit: 'a bridge which is available for all the public may undoubtedly be a charity and it is indifferent how many people use it. But confine its use to a selected number of persons, *however numerous and important*: it is then clearly not a charity. It is not of general public utility: for it does not serve the public purpose *which its nature qualifies it to serve*' (592, emphasis added). The class within a class requirement is not actually concerned with public benefit, but forcing settlors not to place any arbitrary limits on their largesse.

4. NON-CHARITABLE PURPOSE TRUSTS

ORTHODOXY, AND WHEN IT MATTERS

Orthodoxy is, of course, that you cannot create a valid non-charitable purpose trust. In practice, this feature of English law most affects people seeking to create non-charitable purpose trusts in a will.

Inter vivos (among the living), if Sal gives money to Tom to be used for a (non-charitable) purpose *x*, and Tom uses the money for that purpose, the fact that Tom will not have held the money on a valid purpose trust will be neither here nor there. If Tom misappropriates the money and uses it for some other purpose, Sal will certainly be able to sue Tom for the value of the money on the basis that Tom has been unjustly enriched – the basis on which Sal gave Tom that money has failed thanks to Tom's misappropriating it. And if Sal wants to argue that Tom held the money on trust for her, that will be possible too. Sal can argue that when she gave the money to Tom, she expected Tom to hold the money on a purpose trust. This trust turned out to be invalid (because non-charitable), with the result that Tom held the money transferred to him by Sal on a resulting trust for Sal. This did not, however, stop Tom from using the money for the purpose for which Sal gave it to him, as Sal will have *consented* to Tom using the money in that way. So Tom held the money on resulting trust for Sal subject to a power (which Sal could revoke at any time) to use the money for the purpose for which Sal gave the money to Tom.

If, then, Sal makes an *inter vivos* transfer of money to Tom to be used for a particular (non-charitable) purpose *x*, Sal will not be able to compel Tom to use the money for that purpose, but Tom will normally be happy to apply the money for that and if Tom shows signs of being unwilling, Sal can always sue for the money (or its value) back. The rule against non-charitable purpose trusts will not therefore unduly affect Sal. Difficulties set in, however, if Sal tries to leave money to Tom in her will to be used for purpose *x*. In such a case, Sal's next of kin (or residuary legatee, if one is identified in the will) will have ample reason to challenge the validity of the transfer to Tom: if it is invalid, then they will obtain the money that Sal wanted Tom to have because Sal's next of kin (or residuary legatee) will inherit anything that Sal did not validly leave in her will. This is why most cases involving the rule against non-charitable trusts arise out of someone trying to create a non-charitable purpose trust in a will: it is in those cases that the rule against such trusts is most likely to be invoked and matter.

THE EXCEPTIONS

The rule that a non-charitable purpose trust will be invalid is subject to a small number of 'anomalous' exceptions (see, generally, Wilde 2022). A non-charitable purpose trust will be valid if it is a trust for: (a) the erection or maintenance of a funerary monument or grave (*Re Hooper* [1932] 1 Ch 38); (b) the saying of masses for the dead in private (*Re Hetherington* [1990] Ch 1, 9); (c) to pay for the care of specific animals (*Re Dean* (1899) 41 Ch D 552).

No one will have standing to force the trustee of one of these trusts to carry out the trust. Instead, the trustee will only be allowed to accept assets under one of these trusts if they have first indicated willingness to comply with the trust: *Pettingall* v *Pettingall* (1842) 11 LJ Ch 176. If the trustee then goes back on their word, the purpose trust will collapse and a resulting trust back to the settlor will arise which will allow that settlor (or more likely their next of kin, as these trusts invariably feature in wills) to sue the errant trustee to recover the trust assets.

It is clear that, unlike a charitable purpose trust, these trusts cannot last forever. Assets held on one of these trusts must be used up within a certain period of time. It is more debatable how long that period is – whether it is (a) 21 years, or (b) the duration of any life in being at the time the trust is created plus 21 years. The case for (b) is that this is the time limit placed on how far into the future someone can acquire an interest under a trust for persons. The case for (a) is that when it comes to a non-charitable purpose trust, which is not a trust for persons, it makes no sense to make its lifetime dependent on the duration of a life in being at the time the trust is created. (For discussion, see Baxendale-Walker 1999, 101–13.)

It is said that these exceptions to the rule against non-charitable purpose trusts are inexplicable (*Re Endacott* [1960] 1 Ch 232, 250 (per Harman LJ)) or 'concessions to human weakness or sentiment' (*Re Astor* [1952] 1 Ch 534, 547 (per Roxburgh J)), but in fact the reason for recognising these purpose trusts as valid is obvious. Consumer demand requires that they be given effect to: people will not be put off inserting these kinds of provisions into their wills by a threat that they will be held to be invalid. Ensuring that their souls are saved, their graves are tended, and their pets looked after makes it unthinkable for people not to make provisions to this effect in their will (see Moffat 2020, 223).

Consumer demand *might* have led to the creation of a further exception to the rule against non-charitable purpose trusts in the case where someone donates money to a club or society that is unincorporated, and being unincorporated, has no legal existence and cannot be the object of donations. The law *could* have said that because people's loyalties to clubs and societies that have played a large part in their lives mean that they cannot be stopped from making donations to those associations, it will recognise that such donations are made to the treasurer of the association and are held on a valid, though non-charitable, purpose trust – the purpose of the trust being whatever the purpose of the donation was. However, that route was closed off when *Re Endacott* ruled that no further exceptions to the rule against non-charitable purpose trusts would be recognised. Instead, the courts have had to cast around for other devices of recognising the donation as valid, while doing something to ensure that the donor's intentions in making the donation are respected.

It might be possible to pull the trick of saying that the money was given on an invalid purpose trust and is therefore held on a resulting trust for the donor subject to a power to use the donation for the purpose for which it was given. However, this trick will do no good where the donation was made in a will (the deceased's next of kin or residuary legatee will simply claim the donation as held on trust for them) and, as we have seen, a non-charitable purpose trust is most likely to run into trouble when it is created in a will. Similarly with the analysis that the donor retains legal title to the donated money and makes the treasurer of the association his agent, empowering the treasurer to apply the money for the purpose for which it was given (*Conservative Central Office* v *Burrell* [1982] 1 WLR 522). That analysis cannot work where money is given to an unincorporated association in a will (you can't make people your agents after you are dead) despite its being asserted that 'the answer [to this problem] is not hard to find' (ibid, 530 (per Brightman LJ)).

The best the courts have been able to do in the case of donations to an unincorporated association in a will is to say that the donated money is given to the treasurer to be held on trust for the members of the association. But how then do you stop an individual member leaving the association and claiming their share of the donated money? You say that the money is held on trust for the members 'subject to the contract' that exists between the members (*Neville Estates* v *Madden* [1962] Ch 832). That 'contract' (completely fictional in legal reality) will be constituted by the rules of the association, and it will expressly or impliedly provide that an individual member who resigns from the association forfeits any claims they might have in respect of donations to the association. However, analysing donations to an unincorporated association as being held on trust for the members 'subject to the contract' between them is unsatisfactory where:

(1)   money is given to an 'outward-looking' association, which exists for some abstract purpose such as campaigning for some political cause (what is to stop all the members dissolving their 'contract' and the association and going on to split the donations between them?);

(2)   money is given to an 'inward-looking' association, which exists for the benefit of its members, but for a more limited purpose

(the 'contract' between the members will not require them to use such a donation for the purpose for which it was given, but will instead allow them to apply it for the general purposes of the association); and

(3) money is given to an association where under the rules of the association, the members have no say in how that money is used (how can the money be said to be held on trust for the members when they have no rights in relation to that money?).

The difficulties the courts face in such cases could be avoided were they to recognise a new exception to the rule against non-charitable purpose trusts, applying in the case of donations to an unincorporated association. But it seems the courts would rather twist and turn in face of those difficulties than take the easy way out of recognising a new exception.

THE ROAD NOT TAKEN

But it was not always thus. It seems clear that in the late 1960s and early 1970s there was some general dissatisfaction among the judges with the state of the law on non-charitable purpose trusts, and an inclination to start adopting a more liberal approach to recognising such trusts as being valid. This is made clear by the following timeline:

1969: as we have seen, in *Re Denley* [1969] 1 Ch 373, Goff J suggested that a non-charitable purpose trust might be valid if there existed individuals who would benefit from performance of the trust to such an extent that they could be given standing to enforce it. As a result, he held that a trust of land under which the trustees were required to use the land as a 'recreation or sports ground primarily for the benefit of the employees of [a named company] and secondarily for the benefit of such other person or persons (if any) as the trustees may allow to use the same' was perfectly valid.

1970: in *Barclays Bank* v *Quistclose Investments* [1970] AC 567, the House of Lords had to decide what to make of the situation where Quistclose Investments ('QI') loaned £200,000 to Rolls Razor Ltd ('RR') solely for the purpose of paying a dividend to its shareholders (so as to convince various third parties that it was in good financial health) and then RR went into liquidation before the loan money was paid out to

RR's shareholders. Lord Wilberforce held (at 581–82) that when RR had received the loan money from QI, RR had held that money on a 'primary trust' requiring RR to pay that money to its shareholders. When that 'primary trust' failed on RR's going into liquidation, a 'secondary trust' arose whereby RR held the loan money on trust for QI.

Lord Wilberforce's primary trust looks a lot like a purpose trust – a trust to pay money to a third party *so as to convince people of RR's financial health* – which fails when it becomes impossible to convince other people that RR is financially healthy because RR has gone into liquidation. To find that there existed a valid non-charitable purpose trust of this type goes well beyond the 'anomalous' categories of valid non-charitable purpose trusts, and well beyond *Re Denley* (though see Baxendale-Walker 1999, arguing (at 42–50 and 85) that it used to be accepted as elementary that money could be held on a purpose trust to pay off one's creditors).

1971: as we will see in the next chapter, in *McPhail* v *Doulton* [1971] AC 424, the House of Lords (Lord Wilberforce again) opened the door to discretionary trusts for extremely large classes of people to be recognised as valid. As we have already seen, discretionary trusts for extremely large classes have a lot more in common with purpose trusts than do they do with trusts for persons.

1972: in *Dingle* v *Turner* [1972] AC 601, Lord Cross observed (at 624) that 'the question of whether a trust to further some purpose is so little likely to benefit the public that it ought to be declared invalid and the question whether it is likely to confer such great benefit on the public that it should enjoy fiscal immunity are really two quite different questions. The logical solution would be to separate them …'. On this view the question of whether a purpose trust was valid would become separated from the question of whether it was charitable (and therefore deserved tax breaks) – thus opening the door to large numbers of admittedly non-charitable purpose trusts being declared to be valid.

Rightly or wrongly (we will conclude rightly) nothing came of these cases, which had the potential to revolutionise English trusts law. (Though see Parkinson 2002, 660–63, for the view that this potential has been realised.) Instead, in an almost Orwellian rewriting of history, cases like *Denley* and *Quistclose* have been interpreted as saying nothing new, while the implications of Lord Wilberforce's judgment in *McPhail* and Lord Cross's in *Dingle* v *Turner* for purpose trusts are passed over in silence. How did this happen, and why?

ORTHODOXY REASSERTED

Re Denley was the first to go.

In *Re Lipinski's Will Trusts* [1976] 1 Ch 235, money was given to an unincorporated association for the sole purpose of constructing and maintaining buildings for the association. Oliver J endorsed *Re Denley* as according 'both with authority and with common sense' (248) but then went on to make it clear that he interpreted *Re Denley* as holding that a trust intended to benefit persons would be valid as a trust *for persons* even if there was a super-added direction as to how those persons were to be benefited: 'The beneficiaries, the members of the association for the time being, are the persons who could enforce the purpose and they must, as it seems to me, be entitled not to enforce it or, indeed to vary it' (250).

This reading of the trust in *Re Denley* – as a trust for persons, not a purpose trust – was endorsed by Vinelott J in *Re Grant's Will Trusts* [1980] 1 WLR 360, who held that *Re Denley* fell 'altogether outside ... [the law on] purpose trusts' and that the trust in *Re Denley* was a form of discretionary trust – there being 'no distinction in principle between a trust to permit a class ... to use and enjoy land in accordance with rules to be made at the discretion of trustees on the one hand, and on the other hand, a trust to distribute income at the discretion of trustees amongst a class' (370). A generation later, in *Re Horley Town Football Club* [2006] EWHC 2386 (Ch), this fairly extraordinary reading of *Re Denley* was endorsed as though it were obvious (at [47]), though some unease was expressed at the idea of the 'beneficiaries' under a *Re Denley* trust being able to combine together and claim the trust assets under the rule in *Saunders* v *Vautier* when those assets had been plainly intended not to be divided up among the beneficiaries ([99], [131]).

Lord Wilberforce's 'primary trust' in *Quistclose* lasted a little longer. In *Carreras Rothmans Ltd* v *Freeman Matthews Treasure Ltd* [1985] 1 Ch 207, Peter Gibson J held that Lord Wilberforce's primary trust had no beneficiaries ('the beneficial interest is in suspense' until the trust is discharged (223)): a sure sign that the primary trust is a purpose trust. The losing counsel in that case was Peter Millett QC. Never one to accept defeat, Millett turned his arguments in the case into an article on 'The *Quistclose* trust: who can enforce it?' that was published in the *Law Quarterly Review* (Millett 1985). Millett argued that there was no such thing as a primary trust or a secondary trust in a *Quistclose* situation: where Sal loaned money to Tom to be used only for a particular purpose, Tom would *always* hold that money on trust for Sal subject to a power to use it for the purpose for which Sal had loaned the money to Tom. Lord Millett, as he then became, took the chance in *Twinsectra Ltd* v *Yardley* [2002] 2 AC 164 to criticise *Carreras Rothman*'s analysis of the *Quistclose* trust for its 'unorthodoxy' and for failing 'to have regard to' *his* analysis of the *Quistclose* trust as being a straightforward resulting trust for the lender ([90]) – which analysis, he went on to observe, must be correct as all other contending analyses were 'impossible' ([100]).

William Swadling has criticised Millett's analysis as giving the lender multiple rights against the borrower – both under the contract and trusts law – and as giving the lender rights to the return of the loan money (under *Saunders* v *Vautier*) that are inconsistent with the borrower's contractual rights (Swadling 2004, 28). This last point would prove fatal to Millett's analysis if he thought that the resulting trust back to the lender arose because that was what was *intended* (see Smolyansky 2010, 560–62). However, it is possible to argue (though this is not an argument that Millett himself makes: for his final word on the subject, see Millett 2011) that the resulting trust arises out of trust failure: Sal lent money to Tom intending it to be held on a purpose trust that was invalid because non-charitable, with the result that Tom held the money on a resulting trust for Sal (subject of course to a power to apply the money for the purpose for which it had been lent by Sal).

THE USES OF ORTHODOXY

Developments such as these had the effect of killing stone dead whatever might have been trying to flower in the field of the law on non-charitable purpose trusts at the end of the 1960s and the start of the 1970s. Instead, it was left to other jurisdictions to cultivate this field, with jurisdictions such as Bermuda, Jersey and the Cayman Islands all allowing settlors from the 1990s onwards to settle wealth in their jurisdictions on non-charitable purposes trusts that are enforced by a 'protector' (see, generally, Baxendale-Walker 1999, chs 7–10), while the Scottish government is currently proposing to go down the same road: Trusts and Succession (Scotland) Bill 2022, Chapters 6 and 7.

It may be that English law did not go down a similar road in the 1970s because judges who had been weaned on cases like *Re Astor* and *Re Shaw* were simply unable to see the alternative road that *Re Denley* and *Quistclose* were inviting them to travel. However, it may also be that they had a justifiable fear of going down that road. Liberalising the law on non-charitable purpose trusts gives rise to three problems (see, generally, Matthews 1996), which the return to orthodoxy in the 1970s and 1980s allowed English law to avoid.

The first problem is that recognising non-charitable purpose trusts as valid makes tax avoidance (note, not tax *evasion* – which is illegal) far easier. Assets which are held on a purpose trust are not owned beneficially by anyone, which makes income earned by those assets far harder to tax; it is no accident that all the jurisdictions that provide settlors facilities to create valid non-charitable purpose trusts are notorious tax havens. Encouraging tax avoidance might not have been a particularly appetising project for judges living through the kind of economic troubles that the UK experienced in the 1970s (see Whitehead 1985). We will say more about this in chapter five.

The second is that tying up property to be held on a purpose trust is highly likely to be economically inefficient. Think about the trust in *Re Denley*, which was specified to last for '21 years from the death of the last survivor' of a group of people named in the trust deed. While devoting land to a sports ground for the use of employees of a company is undoubtedly admirable – and that may have resulted in Goff J bending over backwards to find the trust in *Re Denley* valid – there is no reason to think that that will be the *best* use of that land, particularly over such a long period of time.

The third is that some kind of quality control would have to be exercised over what kinds of non-charitable purpose trusts will be regarded as valid in order to avoid giving effect to the kind of 'useless' trusts represented by the trust in *Brown v Burdett* (1882) 21 Ch D 667, mentioned in the last chapter. But it would be very difficult for the courts to decide what sort of non-charitable purpose trusts are too 'capricious' (in the sense of pointless) to enforce.

3

Intended and Imposed

1. THE DISTINCTION

The distinction that was the subject matter of the last chapter neatly divides all trusts into two groups – all trusts are either trusts for persons or trusts for purposes. In this chapter we look at a different way of dividing trusts up, into trusts that are intended and trusts that are imposed.

As should be obvious, this distinction refers to why a trust has arisen: all trusts arise because they are either intended or because they are imposed. An intended trust arises because the law empowers people to create trusts and a settlor has exercised that power effectively to create a trust. An imposed trust arises because there are occasions where the law seeks to remedy a problem by finding that certain assets are held on trust for an individual. (All imposed trusts are trusts for persons, while an intended trust can be for a person or a purpose.) Another term for an imposed trust might be a 'remedial' trust – but using that term would create confusion. Imposed trusts are remedial in *function* in that they exist to remedy a problem. But they are *not* remedial in *nature* in that a claimant does *not* have to go to court in order for an imposed trust to arise, when a claimant does have to go court in order to obtain a remedy like an injunction or an order that they be paid damages (see, generally, Birks 1998).

How does this distinction map across to the conventional division of trusts (reflected in s 53 of the Law of Property Act 1925) as being *express, implied, resulting or constructive*? We can immediately see a problem with this division that does not afflict our division of trusts into intended or imposed. If the division 'express, implied, resulting or constructive' aims – as ours does – to refer to *why* a trust arises, the category 'resulting' sticks out like a sore thumb. 'Resulting' seems to refer to what a trust looks like – Tom holds assets on a resulting trust for Ben if he derived those assets from Ben – and not to why it has arisen. Having 'resulting' in this division is akin to dividing Shakespeare plays into comedies, histories, plays with a fool, and tragedies. *King Lear* and *Twelfth Night* do not know where to go in this division – both feature a fool while the first is a tragedy and the second a comedy.

We could make space for 'resulting' in the classification 'express, implied, resulting or constructive' by (1) defining a resulting trust as existing where Tom holds assets on trust for Ben *and* Tom derived those assets from Ben *and* the trust is neither express nor implied and (2) (as we did in the previous chapter) defining a constructive trust as existing where Tom holds assets on trust for Ben *and* Tom did not derive those assets from Ben *and* the trust is neither express nor implied. But it is hard to see any point in doing this other than a conservative wish to hang on to the traditional division of trusts as 'express, implied, resulting or constructive' in the teeth of its being obvious that this division does not work. It would be better to junk the category 'resulting' from this division, which leaves us dividing trusts as being 'express, implied or constructive'. 'Implied' trusts can also go as no one seems to know what they are or have any need to refer to them (William Swadling says they 'have fallen into disuse': Swadling 2013b, 215 n 240) – which then leaves us dividing trusts as being either 'express or constructive'.

This distinction seems to map neatly on to our division of trusts as 'intended or imposed'. But there are three reasons for preferring to divide trusts as 'intended or imposed' rather than 'express or constructive'. The first is that our division is less obscure. In particular, the term 'constructive' is capable of bearing multiple meanings. Sometimes it means 'imposed' but sometimes it means 'fictional' (as in pretending that a dog is a cat by calling the dog a 'constructive cat' (Birks 1989, 22)): see Smith 1999. Our division avoids all such ambiguity. Second, as we will see, the best analysis of trusts that arise out of trust failure is that they are almost always 'imposed' – but such trusts are *not* commonly said to be 'constructive'. Third, as we saw in chapter one, if Ben makes a gift of land to Tom, the law will normally presume that Ben intended that Tom should hold that land on trust for him. If that presumption is not rebutted, then the law will find that Tom holds the land on trust for Ben. That trust is an intended trust – the trust arises out of the law's giving effect to the intention that it presumes Ben had to create a trust – but it would not be usual to call it an 'express' trust, because Ben's intention that Tom hold on trust for him was presumed, not expressed.

2. INTENDED TRUSTS

For an intended trust to arise: (1) the settlor needs to have *intended* to create a trust; (2) the trust assets need to be *vested* in the intended trustee of the trust; (3) the subject matter and objects of the trust need to be sufficiently *certain* for the intended trustee to be able to give effect to the terms of the trust; and (4) any requisite *formalities* need to be observed.

INTENTION TO CREATE A TRUST

The significant role trusts have played in a domestic context means that trusts law has never employed the same presumption *against* finding an intent to create a trust between family members that it does when it comes to finding an intent to create a contract between family members (*Balfour* v *Balfour* [1919] 2 KB 571).

At the same time, if Ben gratuitously transfers land to Tom, the courts will *not* presume *that* Ben intended Tom to hold the land on trust for him if they were married or engaged at the time, or Tom was Ben's son. The most natural inference in such a case will be that Ben intended to make an outright gift of the land to Tom. The fact that the courts will not presume a trust was intended in this sort of case is often said to be due to the courts' relying on a 'presumption of advancement'. However, William Swadling has convincingly argued that there is no such thing: Swadling 2013a. The absence of a presumption that a trust was intended does not amount to a presumption that no trust was intended. It follows that when s 199(1) of the Equality Act 2010 provided that 'The presumption of advancement … is abolished' it was attempting to abolish something that never existed in the first place and consequently could not have any effect on this area of the law. (Perhaps for this reason s 199(1) has never come into force.)

In domestic cases where no presumption that a trust was intended applies, the courts will not lightly find that the owner of assets intended to create a trust over them – even when their failing to do so has dire consequences. In *Jones* v *Lock* (1865) 1 Ch App 25, Jones was a businessman who had been away for a few days. On coming home, he made great play of putting a cheque in his new-born baby's hands, saying that the cheque was for him, and then putting it away in a safe 'for the baby'. It appeared

Jones intended to invest the cheque and £100 of his savings for the benefit of the baby, but he died before he could do this. Even worse, he died without having had a chance to make a new will that would provide for his baby. A claim that Jones had intended to declare that he held the cheque on trust for the baby was rejected: it would be 'very dangerous … if loose conversations' (29) were held to amount to a declaration of trust. But repeated conversations between Sal and Ben where Sal says that the money in a bank account is as much Ben's as it is Sal's will be enough to establish an intent to declare that the bank account is held trust for Sal and Ben in equal shares: *Paul* v *Constance* [1977] 1 WLR 527.

VESTING

We already saw in chapter one an example of the rule that the trust assets must be vested in the intended trustee for a trust to arise: the 'no recharacterisation' rule in *Milroy* v *Lord* (1862) 4 De GF & J 264 says that if Sal intends to transfer assets to Tom that Tom will then hold on trust for Ben, but the transfer of assets to Tom does not go through, no trust will arise. The law will not say that Sal intended to hold those assets on trust for Ben herself and as a result find that Sal holds those assets on trust for Ben. So if Sal does end up holding the assets on trust for Ben (and we will see below that there are occasions when this will happen), that trust is an imposed trust, not an intended trust. In *Choithram* v *Pagarani* [2001] 1 WLR 1, the Privy Council placed a small gloss on this rule: if Sal intends to transfer assets to Sal, Cat, Dan and Eve, so that they will together hold those assets on trust for Ben, but Sal is unable to transfer the assets before she dies, Sal will still hold those assets on an intended trust for Ben. The fact that Sal intended to hold the assets on trust for Ben will be enough to bring the trust into existence, even though Sal only intended to hold those assets on trust for Ben along with Cat, Dan and Eve.

CERTAINTY

For the most part, the rules around the necessary degree of certainty as to the subject matter and objects of a trust can be simply reduced down to one question: Is enough known about the subject matter and objects of the trust to give effect to it?

For example, in *Re Barlow* [1979] 1 WLR 278, Helen Barlow's will provided that paintings belonging to Barlow that she had not left to anyone in her will should be held on trust by her executors to sell them, with any of 'family and friends' having the right to buy paintings at a fixed, discounted, price. The direction in relation to family and friends was held to be perfectly valid because the executors knew enough to give effect to it: 'In order to decide whether an individual is entitled to purchase, all that is required is that the executors should be able to say of that individual whether he has proved that he is a friend' or a member of Barlow's family (282) – and there would clearly be cases where someone could prove that this was the case.

Similarly, in *Boyce* v *Boyce* (1849) 16 Sim 476 (discussed, Wilde 2020), Richard Boyce's will left all his houses on trust for his wife for life, and further provided that on his wife's death, his trustees should convey to his daughter Maria whichever house she should choose, with the other houses going to his daughter Charlotte. Unfortunately, having made this will, all of Boyce's immediate family except for Charlotte died – and Boyce did not make another will to take account of this fact. When Boyce died, Boyce's grandchild argued that the trust in Boyce's will had failed, with the result he should inherit everything. The court agreed: Boyce's trustees could not give Charlotte any houses under the will because they did not know which houses to give her as Maria had never made a choice of which house she wanted.

While most of the cases on the requisite degree of certainty of subject matter and objects needed under a trust give effect to the simple question, 'Is enough known about the subject matter and objects of the trust to give effect to it?' the courts have sometimes departed from this straightforward approach, with unfortunate results.

(1) *Shares.* In *Hunter* v *Moss* [1994] 1 WLR 452, Moss declared that he held 50 of his 950 shares in Moss Electrical Co Ltd ('MEL') on trust for Hunter, so as to give Hunter a 5 per cent stake in the company (which had a total issued share capital of 1,000 shares). The Court of Appeal held that this was a valid declaration of trust, even though it was not made clear which of Moss's 950 shares were intended to be held on trust for Hunter. It was therefore not possible to know how to give effect to the trust declared by Moss.

The Court of Appeal said this was not a problem as had Moss's will left Hunter 50 of his 950 shares in MEL, that provision would have been valid (457). But in such a case the executors of Moss's will would have known enough to give effect to this provision – they would have known what they had to do was take *any* 50 shares from Moss's holding and transfer them to Hunter. But it was not the case in *Hunter* v *Moss* that any 50 shares could be held on trust for Hunter – we would have to know *which* 50 shares were held on trust, in order to know, for example, whether when Moss sold 500 shares in MEL, the 50 shares held on trust for Hunter were included in the sale or not.

It has been argued (Goode 2018, 119–29; Stevens 2017, 119) that because shares cannot be segregated, the decision in *Hunter* v *Moss* was right. It is only a convenience of language that makes us think that Moss had 950 shares in MEL. He was in fact a co-owner of MEL, with a 95 per cent interest in the company. Moss's declaration of trust was over the entirety of that 95 per cent interest, so that Moss held that interest on trust for himself and Hunter as to just under 90 per cent for Moss and just over 5 per cent for Hunter. This is how *Hunter* v *Moss* has been subsequently interpreted (*Re Lehman Brothers International (Europe)* [2011] EWCA Civ 1544, [69]–[74]) and while it's obvious that the maths involved in adopting this approach has the potential to get supremely complicated very quickly, *Hunter* is now the foundation of a multi-million-pound industry in intermediated securities and as a result it is impossible that it can now be overruled.

(2) *'Anything left'* trusts. It is clear as anything can be in the law that a provision in a will leaving 'the rest of my estate' to Ron will be valid. The will's executors will know enough to be able to give effect to this provision – Ron gets whatever is left once the rest of the estate has been distributed in accordance with the terms of the will. But a different kind of provision ran into trouble in *Sprange* v *Barnard* (1789) 2 Bro CC 585. Susannah Sprange left £300 worth of securities to her husband 'for his sole use, and at his death, the remaining part of what is left, that he does not want for his own wants and use' should go to her siblings. It was held this amounted to an outright gift of the securities to her husband: the 'anything left' provision could not be given effect to because it was impossible to tell *here and now* what kind of interest, if any, the siblings had in the securities. But it is not clear why we would need to tell here and now what interest the siblings had, instead of waiting to see what was left at the death of the husband. This 'wait and see' approach seems to have been adopted by the Court of Appeal in *Ottaway* v *Norman* [1972]

Ch 698, under which approach the siblings in *Sprange* would be conceived as having rights 'floating' over the securities left in their sister's will to their brother-in-law, with those rights only crystallising in relation to whatever was left once the brother-in-law died.

(3) *Discretionary trusts.* The leading case on the requirement of certainty of objects in relation to discretionary trusts is the House of Lords' decision in *McPhail* v *Doulton* [1971] AC 424. Lord Wilberforce gave the judgment of the majority (with which Lord Reid and Viscount Dilhorne agreed; Lords Hodson and Guest dissented). Like an inconsistent three-act play, Lord Wilberforce's judgment has a good beginning, a weak middle, and a clever (but much misunderstood) ending.

The good beginning (449): consistently with the opening of this section, Lord Wilberforce observed that the traditional requirement that it be possible to draw up a complete list of the potential beneficiaries under a discretionary trust made no sense. We don't need to be able to draw up a complete list of potential beneficiaries in order to give effect to a discretionary trust: 'a trustee with a duty to distribute, particularly among a potentially very large class, would surely never require the preparation of a complete list of names, which anyhow would tell him little that he needs to know. He would examine the field, by class and category ...'.

The weak middle (456): 'the test for the validity of [discretionary trusts] ought to be ... that the trust is valid if it can be said with certainty that any given individual is or is not a member of the class' of beneficiaries to be considered under the discretionary trust. We will come back to why this 'is or is not' test for the certainty of objects under a discretionary trust is regrettable.

The clever ending (457): by committing to the 'is or is not' test – under which a discretionary trust would be valid if it is possible to tell of any given individual whether they or do not fall within the class of beneficiaries to be considered – Lord Wilberforce realised that he had opened the door to discretionary trusts for very large classes of people (even a discretionary trust for everyone in the world) to be declared to be valid. He had done so on the basis that it was not necessary to have a complete list of potential beneficiaries to give effect to the trust – which, in the context of a discretionary trust, means giving effect to the intentions of the settlor in setting up the trust.

But Lord Wilberforce must also have realised that there may be occasions where a discretionary trust for a very large class of people *would* need a complete list of potential beneficiaries to be given effect to. This is where the intentions of the settlor in setting up the trust could only be given effect to by equal distribution of the trust assets among all the potential beneficiaries. Lord Wilberforce's judgment created a trap for trustees of such a trust: the trust would be regarded as valid but they would be unable to give effect to it because the class of potential beneficiaries under the trust would be so large that equal distribution among all the beneficiaries would be impossible. To help those trustees out, Lord Wilberforce created an escape hatch for them: they could argue that the discretionary trust is invalid because it 'is administratively unworkable or in Lord Eldon's words one that cannot be executed (*Morice* v *Bishop of Durham*, 10 Ves Jr 522, 527).'

(This last aspect of Lord Wilberforce's judgment has never been properly understood. For example, it has been suggested that a discretionary trust will be invalid for 'administrative unworkability' where the class of potential beneficiaries under the trust is 'far too large' (*R* v *District Auditor, ex p West Yorkshire Metropolitan County Council* (1986) 26 RVR 24, 26 (per Lloyd LJ)). But a discretionary trust for millions of people is still perfectly workable if the trustee examines 'the field, by class and category' – and the trust in the *West Yorkshire* case (which *was* invalidated for administrative unworkability) was perfectly workable as it was intended to replicate the functions of a council that was about to be abolished.)

The weakness in Lord Wilberforce's judgment is its endorsement of the 'is or is not' test for the validity of a discretionary trust. Just as it is not necessary to draw up a complete list of potential beneficiaries under a discretionary trust for the trust to be valid, neither is it necessary to know of any given individual in the world whether they do or do not fall within the class to be considered. In order to give effect to the intentions of the settlor in setting up the discretionary trust, it is not necessary to survey the entirety of the class identified by the settlor: it is 'sufficient if a core class is surveyed' (Swadling 2013b, 220). It should be enough, then, if the definition of the class of potential beneficiaries under a discretionary trust is such that 'if, as regards at least a substantial number of objects, it can be said with certainty that they fall within the trust'.

Those words are taken from Megaw LJ's judgment in the sequel to *McPhail* v *Doulton* – *Re Baden (No 2)* [1973] Ch 9 (at 24) – where the Court of Appeal had to consider whether a discretionary trust would be invalid where it was not possible to tell of any given individual whether they fell within or without the class of potential beneficiaries not because of any vagueness (or 'conceptual uncertainty') in the definition of the class, but because of practical evidential difficulties in determining whether a given individual fell inside or outside the class (or 'evidential uncertainty'). The Court of Appeal ruled by two to one (Sachs LJ agreeing with Megaw LJ on this point) that evidential uncertainty would not invalidate a discretionary trust. But it remains the case that conceptual uncertainty *will* invalidate a discretionary trust so that a discretionary trust for the settlor's 'friends' will be invalid, even if it is perfectly possible to tell of a 'substantial number' of people that they were clearly friends of the settlor. The settlor would have been perfectly happy for the trustees to focus on benefiting that 'core class' of friends – but the trust will still fail just because there will be other people who we cannot tell whether to say they are friends of the settlor or not because the concept of a 'friend' is inherently vague. (Note that *Re Barlow*, discussed above, does not say anything different. That was a case of a fixed trust for 'family and friends' where uncertainty around the concept of who is a friend did not invalidate the trust, as the trust would be valid provided that at least one person could show that they were *clearly* a friend (which some people obviously could).)

(4) *Uncertainty-curing clauses.* What if our settlor tries to help out the trustees by creating a discretionary trust for 'my friends; in cases of doubt as to whether or not someone is my friend, my wife to decide'? Do the trustees now know enough to be able to give effect to the trust? One would have thought that they did. However, as the decision of the Court of Appeal in *Re Tuck's Settlement Trusts* [1978] Ch 49 shows, the law as to when an uncertainty-curing clause will be effective to validate an otherwise fatally uncertain trust is not clear. That case concerned a trust set up by a Jewish baronet, providing that his heirs should be paid a much-reduced sum under the trust if they marry someone who was not 'of the Jewish faith', with the Chief Rabbi getting to decide in cases of doubt whether an heir had married someone who was 'of the Jewish faith' or not.

Lord Denning MR thought that there was no reason why the settlor should not employ an uncertainty-curing clause to resolve any conceptual uncertainty that might invalidate a trust. On this view, our imaginary trust above would be valid. Eveleigh LJ validated the trust on the ground that it essentially provided that an heir would be disinherited (in part) if they married someone who was 'not, in the opinion of the Chief

Rabbi, of the Jewish faith' where the Chief Rabbi's opinion becomes *part of the definition* of whether the condition for disinheriting the heir is satisfied. As a result, that definition was not uncertain and could not invalidate the trust. On this view, our imaginary trust would only be valid if the same trick could be pulled. If, on the other hand, the opinion of the settlor's wife does *not* form part of the definition of the class to be benefited, then the trust would remain invalid for conceptual uncertainty: *Re Coxen* [1948] Ch 747. Lord Russell of Killowen thought that 'of the Jewish faith' was sufficiently certain as a condition even without the provision as regards the Chief Rabbi, and so the *Re Tuck* trust could not be invalidated on grounds of uncertainty. The same view could not be taken in our imaginary trust above, and it is uncertain whether Lord Russell would have sided with Lord Denning or Eveleigh LJ in such a case.

The better view, it is submitted, is Lord Denning's, subject to two qualifications. First, a discretionary trust for 'people who my trustees think are my friends' should be invalid as it does not put the trustees in any better position in terms of their ability to give effect to the trust than if they were simply told to distribute money among 'my friends': *Re Jones* [1953] Ch 125. Second, what a third party, Téa, has to decide under an uncertainty-curing clause has to be sufficiently certain that Téa's opinion can be set aside where there is evidence that Téa is acting dishonestly or wholly unreasonably in making a decision under that clause: *Dundee General Hospitals Board of Management* v *Walker* [1952] 1 All ER 896. 'My friends' is probably certain enough by this standard; but a discretionary trust for 'all those who share my values; in cases of doubt my wife to decide' would not be.

FORMALITIES

There are no general formalities that need to be observed in order to create a trust.

This is so even in relation to a trust over land. Section 53(1)(b) of the Law of Property Act 1925 merely provides that the courts will not recognise the existence of a trust over land unless it is evidenced in writing. In its original incarnation in s 7 of the Statute of Frauds 1677, this provision was designed to prevent landowners being defrauded of their land by a complete stranger getting eleven people to join the claimant in swearing that they had *heard* the landowner declare he held his land on trust for the claimant, thereby convincing a court to recognise that the land was held on trust for the claimant. So a trust over land *can* arise without the need for writing – it is just that it will be difficult (though, as we will see, not impossible) to get a court to recognise its existence. It follows that if Sal orally declares that she holds Blackacre on trust for Ben, and Ben then demands that Sal hand over title to Blackacre under the rule in *Saunders* v *Vautier*, and Sal complies, Sal will not be able subsequently to reverse the transfer: it was made pursuant to a perfectly valid trust, albeit one that would not be recognised by a court of law (or, back in the day, Equity) were it to be the subject of litigation.

If Sal wants to create a trust for the benefit of Ben after Sal dies the courts have held that Sal is *not* compelled by s 9 of the Wills Act 1837 to include the details of the trust in her will. Sal can instead keep those details secret. It is enough if Sal gets an assurance from Tom that he *will* hold assets on trust for Ben if they are left to him in Sal's will. If Sal's will then specifies that Tom should be given those assets (i) outright, or (ii) to hold 'on trust' (without specifying for whom), then when Tom receives those assets, a *secret trust* for the benefit of Ben will arise '*dehors*' (or outside) the will in line with Sal and Tom's agreement – with the secret trust being called 'fully secret' in (i) and 'half secret' in (ii): *McCormick* v *Grogan* (1869) LR 4 HL 82 (fully secret trust); *Blackwell* v *Blackwell* [1929] AC 318 (half secret trust).

The lack of any need for formality in creating a trust is surprising, for two reasons. First, Lon Fuller's classic essay on 'Consideration and form' identified three functions that are performed by formalities require-ments: (1) an *evidentiary* function, enabling a court or third party to see that a particular legal transaction has been entered into; (2) a *caution-ary* function, encouraging someone entering into a legal transaction to think about what they are doing and the wisdom of doing so; and (3) a *channelling* function, providing someone with a clearly defined way of achieving a particular legal goal: Fuller 1941, 800–04. One would have thought that all these functions would be engaged when someone is exer-cising the power to create a trust. A requirement that a trust be created in writing would provide a clearly defined way of creating a trust, put the settlor on notice that they are doing something that is both legally signifi-cant and (seemingly) contrary to their interests, and provide useful evi-dence in case of future disputes of what the settlor did. But the law does not require a trust to be created in writing. Instead, as Jeffrey Hackney observes, the law allows me to '*informally* transfer to you my economic advantages in chattels of huge value by a few significantly chosen words, and once simply done the act cannot be revoked' (Hackney 1987, 109; emphasis added; see also Agnew and Douglas 2019, 75–79).

Second, the law *does* require that writing be used to dispose of one's rights under a trust to another person: Law of Property Act 1925, s 53(1)(c). So if Tom holds assets on trust for Ben, and Ben instructs Tom to hold those assets on trust for Cat, that instruction will need to be in writing for Tom to hold on trust for Cat; if no writing is used, then Tom will still hold on trust for Ben: *Grey* v *Inland Revenue Commissioners* [1960] AC 1. Why writing is needed to transfer Ben's rights under a trust to Cat, but not for those rights to be created in the first place, is a bit of a mystery. It might be argued that the requirement of writing performs an evidentiary function here. If Ben instructs Tom to hold on trust for Cat and Tom does so, the fact that the instruction has to be in writing to be effective will provide Tom with useful protection should Ben subsequently and conveniently forget that instruction and seek to sue Tom on the basis that Tom is committing a breach of trust by applying the trust assets for Cat's benefit and not Ben's. But this rationale runs into trouble when we consider the House of Lords' decision in *Vandervell* v *Inland Revenue Commissioners* [1967] AC 291.

In that case, 100,000 shares in Vandervell Products Ltd ('VPL') were held on trust for Guy Vandervell, an industrialist who controlled VPL. In 1958, Vandervell orally instructed his trustees to transfer the shares outright to the Royal College of Surgeons ('RCS'), but retain an option to repurchase the shares for £5,000. The idea was that the RCS would fund a chair in pharmacology (which would cost about £150,000) out of the dividends paid on the shares and once they had been paid sufficient monies for that purpose, the shares would come back to Vandervell's trustees. But these dividend payments attracted the attention of the Inland Revenue, who claimed in 1961 that under UK tax law, the dividend payments should be regarded as Vandervell's income with the result that he had to pay tax on them.

The Inland Revenue's first argument in favour of this claim, when the matter finally reached the courts, was that even after the shares in VPL were transferred to the RCS, they were still held on trust for Vandervell. His oral instruction to his trustees to transfer the shares to the RCS was intended to dispose of his rights under the trust to the RCS and was therefore ineffective under s 53(1)(c). The House of Lords rejected this argument: Vandervell's instruction was intended to *destroy* his rights under the trust, not dispose of them (Hackney 1987, 90). Once his instruction was complied with, the shares would not be held on trust for anyone and therefore no one would have the equivalent of the rights Vandervell had before the instruction was carried out.

The effect of this aspect of the decision in *Vandervell* is that if Tom holds assets on trust for Ben and Ben instructs Tom to transfer those assets to Cat so that Cat takes those assets beneficially (or, the same thing in different words, outright) Ben's instruction does not need to be in writing to be perfectly effective. However, this leaves Tom vulnerable to being sued by Ben in exactly the way that s 53(1)(c) (we were supposing) was intended to avoid. If Ben's instruction is not put in writing and Tom acts on it, Ben may conveniently forget the instruction and try to sue Tom, claiming that he has transferred to Cat assets held on trust for Ben without any authority to do so. So either s 53(1)(c) does not, after all, seek to perform an evidentiary function (in which case, why do we have it?), or it does seek to perform that function, but imperfectly so in cases like *Vandervell*.

3. CONSTRUCTIVE TRUSTS

If constructive trusts are trusts, then they undoubtedly fall on the 'imposed' side of our divide between intended and imposed trusts. But are they trusts at all? Until recently, no one would have thought to question the matter – but William Swadling has recently and brilliantly suggested that it is a mistake to think of constructive trusts as being trusts: Swadling 2011. Recall that it was said above (at p 54) that the word 'constructive' had a dual meaning in English law: sometimes it means 'imposed' and sometimes it means 'fictional'. Until Swadling, everyone thought that constructive trusts were imposed trusts. However, Swadling suggests that constructive trusts are fictional trusts – they arise in situations where the courts act *as though* there is a trust, even though none actually exists.

Why would the courts do this? The reason lies in the rule in *Saunders* v *Vautier*, and the power that that rule gives the beneficiary under a trust to demand that the trustee hand over title to the trust assets to the beneficiary. Swadling's argument is that when the courts recognise that Tom holds assets on a constructive trust for Ben, the courts do so *simply* for the purpose of empowering Ben to demand that Tom hand over those assets to Ben. There is no intention that Tom hold the assets for Ben indefinitely and do so subject to all the normal duties of a trustee. If this is the case, it might be objected, why do the courts say that the assets are held on a *constructive trust* for Ben? Why not just say that Ben has a power to demand that Tom hand over those assets? The reason is a problem of language. English law simply does not have a good name for that kind of power, so that it can crisply say *what* Ben has when Ben has that power. Instead, it casts around for a situation where someone will have that power and, seeing that that power will exist under a trust, says that Tom holds assets on a trust for Ben. But because the courts are finding the trust simply in order to endow Ben with a power that a beneficiary under a trust has (instead of finding, as would normally be the case, that Ben has the power because he is a beneficiary under a trust) they call the trust 'constructive'.

If Swadling were correct, then we would have good grounds for thinking that the second category of trusts discussed in this chapter – imposed trusts – is illusory, and that all trusts are intended. However, two objections can be made to his position. First, it could be argued that where Tom holds assets on a constructive trust for Ben, Ben has something more than a mere *power* to demand that Tom transfer the assets to Ben. Tom has a *duty* to hand those assets over, while Ben has a corresponding *right* that Tom transfer those assets to Ben. It is because Tom has that duty (and Ben has that corresponding right) that we are justified in saying that Tom holds the assets on trust for Ben: McFarlane 2010, 186–91. Second, it could be argued that trusts come in many different forms (as we saw in chapter one), and the mere fact that a constructive trust may be a stripped-down version of an intended trust does not give us a good reason to deny that it is a trust at all. As it happens, in terms of how they operate, it is difficult to distinguish between a constructive trust and a bare trust (where Tom holds title to property subject to an obligation to apply that property as Ben directs), and no one denies that a bare trust is properly called a trust.

Having said that, Swadling is right to this extent – when the courts recognise that Tom holds assets on a constructive trust for Ben, their object in doing so is to ensure the transfer of those assets from Tom to Ben. As such, the constructive trust is a tool for bringing about the redistribution of property and we are entitled to feel some unease about that tool being wielded by unelected judges, especially ones who purport to wield it pursuant to their sense of what 'justice and good conscience' require (*Hussey* v *Palmer* [1972] 1 WLR 1286, 1290 (per Lord Denning MR)): see Birks 1994.

This tool can be brought under control and tamed if we say that it will only be used where Tom has a pre-existing duty under the general law to transfer assets to Ben. Indeed, theorists like Ben McFarlane and Robert Stevens – pursuant to their 'right against a right' analysis of a trust (p 13) – would argue that a constructive trust can only be properly recognised as arising in such a situation. In their view, constructive trusts arise as a matter of simple logic. Whenever Ben has rights over Tom's rights there is a trust (as a matter of definition) and if the trust has not been deliberately created so as to bring Ben's rights into existence, the trust must be constructive in nature: it exists by virtue of Ben's *already* having rights over Tom's rights. However, as we will see, the courts have recognised constructive trusts as arising in situations where it cannot conceivably be said that Tom has a pre-existing duty to transfer assets to Ben; we shall have to see whether they acted wisely or legitimately in so doing.

VENDOR-PURCHASER CONSTRUCTIVE TRUSTS ('VPCTs')

As we saw with *Lady Foliamb's Case* in chapter one, VPCTs are probably the oldest examples of constructive trusts (Oakley 1997, 275) and the ones that fit closest to the McFarlane-Stevens view of constructive trusts. They arise in the case where Tom has contractually undertaken to sell an asset to Ben and that undertaking is specifically enforceable. 'Equity will treat as done what ought to be done' and regard Tom as holding the asset on trust for Ben simply by virtue of having contracted to sell that asset to Ben. The asset in question will usually be an interest in land – contracts to buy interests in land are specifically enforceable by virtue of the fact that land is regarded as unique, so that if the contract were breached, damages would not be an adequate remedy.

Contrary to Swadling's thesis, the aim of the VPCT seems not to be to get Tom to transfer to Ben the asset that he has contracted to sell to Ben: Ben's ability to apply to the courts for an order of specific performance would be sufficient for that. Instead, the VPCT exists to provide Ben with certain extra rights that Ben would not have under the Tom-Ben contract alone. As listed by Peter Turner (Turner 2012, 585–86), they are: (i) a right against third parties to the asset that Ben has contracted to buy from Tom; (ii) a right that Tom preserve the asset before the contract is performed; (iii) a right to any profits that Tom might obtain from holding the asset longer than he is supposed to do under the contract; (iv) a lien over the asset for repayment of any money Ben has paid Tom in advance for that asset should Tom not perform. These rights come into existence at various times over the course of the Tom-Ben contract, which lends the VPCT a somewhat mysterious, shape-shifting quality.

IMPERFECT TRANSFERS

If Tom wishes to make a gift of an asset to Ben, but fails to do so, there will be no basis for saving the gift by finding that Tom holds that asset on an *intended* trust for Ben. Under the 'no recharacterization rule' in *Milroy* v *Lord*, Tom's intention to make a gift to Ben cannot be turned into an intention to declare that he holds the subject matter of the gift on trust for Ben. But the courts will sometimes find that Tom *does* hold that subject matter on a *constructive* trust for Ben.

The first occasion is under the 'rule in *Re Rose*', named after *Re Rose* [1952] 1 Ch 499. Eric Rose intended to make a gift of 20,000 shares to his wife, Rosamond. Eric did everything he needed to do to transfer the shares to Rosamond by 30 March 1943, but the transfer only went through on 30 June 1943, as the transfer had to be approved by the directors of the company in which the shares were held. This delay in the transfer of the shares going through proved very significant when Eric died four years later on 16 February 1947. Inheritance tax would be payable on any gifts that Eric made before 10 April 1943 – and the transfer of shares to Rosamond happened after that date.

The Court of Appeal evidently thought it would be very unfair on Rosamond if she had to pay inheritance tax on the 20,000 shares transferred to her just because there had been a delay in registering the transfer of the shares that had nothing to do with either her or Eric. So they wilfully misinterpreted some remarks of Turner LJ in *Milroy* v *Lord* and held that once Eric had done everything *he* needed to do to transfer the 20,000 shares to Rosamond, he held those shares on a constructive trust for her (510–11). So, effectively, by 30 March 1943, Eric no longer owned the shares outright but held them on trust for Rosamond, with the result that she did not have to pay inheritance tax on the shares. This ruling – designed purely to help Rosamond out of having to pay an unfair tax – gave birth to the 'rule in *Re Rose*': if Tom wants to make a gift of assets to Ben and has done everything that he needs to do to transfer those assets to Ben, he will then hold those assets on constructive trust for Ben.

You know the law is in trouble when people start naming rules or other aspects of the law after case names – they are confessing that the case is very hard to make sense of in a principled way. (Witness 'the rule in *Saunders* v *Vautier*' or 'the *Quistclose* trust'.) That is true *par excellence* of the 'rule in *Re Rose*' – it is impossible to find any clear rationale for it (though see Liew 2017, 205–11). But at least the rule has the merit of only applying in very limited circumstances. The same cannot be said of 'the trust in *Pennington* v *Waine*'.

In *Pennington* v *Waine* [2002] 1 WLR 2075, Ada Crampton owned 1,500 shares in a company created by her husband and his brother (her brother-in-law). Her brother-in-law owned 500 shares in the company. On 30 September 1998, Ada told the company accountant that she wanted to transfer 400 of her shares in the company to her nephew, Harold – the son of Ada's brother-in-law. A share transfer form was filled out the same day, but it was filed away by the company accountant, and nothing was done with it. But both Ada and Harold believed that he was now the owner of 400 shares in the company, which allowed him to become a director of the company. Ada then made a will on 10 November 1998 under which she left 620 shares in the company to Harold. Together with the 400 shares she assumed she had already transferred to Harold, that would give Harold 1,020 shares in the company – a 51 per cent holding and therefore majority control. Ada then died on 19 November 1998, thinking that she had ensured that Harold would have control over her husband's company for the foreseeable future. But the 400 shares had not been transferred to Harold. Ada's executors went to court to find out what was the status of those shares. Were they held on trust for Harold or were they still held beneficially by Ada? If the latter, the shares would be sold, along with the rest of Ada's belongings, to fund a number of different bequests made in her will – and Harold would only have a 31 per cent stake in the company that Ada had wanted him to control.

If we step back a bit, the facts of *Pennington* are on all fours with the kind of situation that tort law attempts to remedy by finding a duty of care under *White* v *Jones* [1995] 2 AC 207. Ada wants to make a gift to

Harold. She seeks the help of the company accountant to make the gift. Due to his neglect the gift is not made. And then Ada's death prevents her from remedying the situation. On those facts, the accountant would have owed Harold a duty of care under *White* v *Jones*, and Harold could have sued the accountant in negligence for the fact that he did not receive the 400 shares, and majority control of the company.

So the courts had already indicated before *Pennington* that they were willing to intervene to provide some kind of remedy in that kind of case. Given this, it is no surprise that the Court of Appeal in *Pennington* went out of its way to protect Harold's interests, not by giving him a claim in tort against the company accountant, but by finding that Ada's 400 shares were held on trust for Harold; a trust that was necessarily constructive as Ada never intended to hold those shares on trust for Harold. (Interestingly, the leading judgment in *Pennington* was given by Arden LJ, who only two years before – as Arden J – applied *White* v *Jones* to find a firm of solicitors liable for incompetently advising a woman just like Ada as to how to give shares in a company she controlled to nieces and nephews just like Harold without surrendering control of the company or incurring a tax liability: *Estill* v *Cowling, Swift & Kitchin* [2000] Lloyd's Rep PN 378.)

The Court of Appeal could not find a trust by applying the rule in *Re Rose* as Ada had not done everything she needed to do to transfer her shares to Harold ([65]). Instead, and extremely confusingly, they found that Ada's 400 shares were held on trust for Harold because 'a stage was reached where it would have been *unconscionable* for Ada to recall the gift' of the 400 shares ([66], emphasis added). This is confusing for two reasons.

First, the real reason for finding a trust in *Pennington* was that Ada had always wanted Harold to have the shares (see [66], per Arden LJ, and [76], per Clarke LJ), and not that Ada would have done anything wrong by changing her mind about giving Harold the shares. Second, it is hard to argue that Ada would have done something wrong by changing her mind about giving Harold the shares unless Harold *relied* in some way on Ada's assurance that he was now the owner of 400 shares in the company. But Harold did not rely in any way on any such assurance – and the Court of Appeal did not care that he had not relied because, as has just been observed, the real basis of the trust in *Pennington* v *Waine* was that Ada always wanted Harold to have the shares and was prevented from giving them to Harold by the company accountant.

These confusions have turned the case law interpreting *Pennington* v *Waine* into a mess, with *Curtis* v *Pulbrook* [2011] EWHC 167 (Ch) ruling (at [43]) that reliance is needed for a trust to arise under *Pennington* v *Waine*, while *Khan* v *Mahmood* [2021] EWHC 597 (Ch) says it is not (at [44]). The better view is that the trust in *Pennington* v *Waine* arises where Tom wishes to make a gift of assets to Ben and seeks Cat's assistance to make that gift, and is then prevented from doing so by Cat's fault. No reliance by Ben is required for the trust to arise, but neither is the basis of the trust the fact that Tom would act unconscionably by going back on his intention to make a gift. Indeed, one situation where the trust would *not* arise is where, despite Cat's fault, Tom can *still* make a gift of the assets he wished to transfer to Ben, but then chooses not to do so. This was the case in *Khan* v *Mahmood*, which must therefore be regarded as wrongly decided.

THE TRUST IN *ROCHEFOUCAULD v BOUSTEAD*

Here is another trust named after a case, thus indicating the considerable uncertainty surrounding how it should be analysed.

In *Rochefoucauld* v *Boustead* [1897] 1 Ch 196, Emily, the Comtesse de la Rochefoucauld, owned certain coffee plantations in Ceylon, which were managed by Boustead. Emily mortgaged the plantations to the Société Générale, based in Amsterdam. Under the mortgage, the Société got title to the plantations in return for making a very large loan to Emily: if she paid the loan off, she would get the title back. The Société began agitating to be paid back the money it had lent Emily, threating that if the loan were not repaid, it would sell the plantations and recover its money from the proceeds of the sale. Emily did not have the money to pay the Société back, but Boustead offered to help Emily out.

Emily and Boustead's plan was that Boustead would buy the plantations from the Société, thereby paying off the mortgage, and would hold the plantations on trust for Emily, subject only to his having a charge over the plantations for the money he had spent buying them from the Société. Boustead bought the plantations for a lot less than they were actually worth as the Société was only interested in raising enough money from the sale to be paid back how much it had lent Emily. Boustead then proceeded, without Emily's knowledge or consent, to mortgage the plantations multiple times over in order to raise money to pay off his creditors.

When Emily found out, she sued Boustead, claiming that he held the plantations on trust for her and was liable for any gains and losses that had resulted from his dealings with the plantations.

The Court of Appeal found for Emily. It expressly said that Boustead held the plantations on an 'express' trust for Emily (208). Emily could establish the existence of this trust despite her arrangement with Boustead not being put in writing – something that the courts would normally require under s 7 of the Statute of Frauds 1677 (now s 53(1)(b) of the Law of Property Act 1925) if they were to recognise a trust over land. This is because the courts would not allow the Statute of Frauds to be used as an 'instrument of fraud' – and it would be so used if Emily conveyed land to Boustead to be held on trust for her, and Boustead knew the land was being conveyed to him on this basis but was now relying on the Statute of Frauds 'in order to keep the land himself' (206). Despite this, many writers analyse the *Rochefoucauld* trust as being constructive in nature. The trust was imposed, they say, to prevent Boustead gaining an advantage that he was only in a position to make as a result of the promises he made to Emily and that he could only make by breaking those promises (McFarlane 2004, Liew 2017 (58–59), Grower 2021).

While this is an interesting explanation of the case, Occam's Razor (which says that the simpler explanations are more likely to be correct than more complicated ones) demands that we should analyse the *Rochefoucald* trust as being an intended trust (as does Swadling 2010 and Douglas 2021) unless it is impossible to do so. Ying Khai Liew says that this *is* impossible: Emily could not have declared Boustead held the plantations on trust for her as she never had title to them at the relevant time, while Boustead would not have been acting fraudulently if he had orally declared he held the plantations on trust for Emily and then went back on that declaration, relying on the Statute of Frauds to do so (Liew 2017, 42–46). What this overlooks is that the Court of Appeal held that Boustead purchased the plantations '*as a trustee*' for Emily (212, emphasis added). This suggests that Boustead was already a trustee when he purchased the plantations. But what was he a trustee of? The answer must be – the purchase money used to buy the plantations. Boustead was perfectly entitled to declare that he held that money on trust for Emily without any formality, and if he held that money on an intended trust for Emily then it follows very straightforwardly that the plantations purchased with that money were also held on an intended trust for Emily.

COMMON INTENTION CONSTRUCTIVE TRUSTS

Rochefoucauld is taken as authority for the proposition that if Tom purchases land from Ben on the understanding that Tom will hold that land on trust for Ben, Tom will hold the land on (an intended) trust for Ben even if the understanding is not put in writing: *Bannister v Bannister* [1948] 2 All ER 133. But how can Ben informally acquire rights over Blackacre when Tom acquired Blackacre from someone else?

In a rational system of law, two ways would suggest themselves: (1) Ben contributed monetarily to the purchase of Blackacre, in which case Tom would hold his rights over Blackacre on trust for himself and Ben in proportion to their respective contributions to the acquisition of those rights under a *Dyer* v *Dyer*-style presumed resulting trust; or (2) Tom assured Ben that Blackacre was or would be held on trust for him in some proportion and Ben relied on that assurance, in which case Tom would hold his rights over Blackacre on trust for Ben to whatever extent was necessary to ensure that Ben was not made any worse off as a result of relying on Tom's assurances, though not to any greater extent than Ben was initially promised by Tom.

These two ways of informally acquiring trust rights over Blackacre are very different. The trust that arises by way of route (1) is an intended trust (where the intention to create a trust is presumed), while the trust that arises by way of route (2) is an imposed (constructive) trust. Unfortunately, in *Gissing* v *Gissing* [1971] AC 886, Lord Diplock indulged the common lawyer's characteristic penchant for monomania (trying to reduce everything down to just one thing) by trying to suggest that (1) and (2) are each manifestations of the *same thing* – what has come to be known as a 'common intention constructive trust'. This trust arises where Tom 'by his words or conduct … has induced [Ben] to act to his own detriment in the reasonable belief that by so acting [he] was acquiring a beneficial interest in the land' (905). Where (2) is true this is obviously made out, but how does Lord Diplock's formulation cover (1)? (1) is covered, he claimed, because in that case we can *infer* from Ben's contributing to the purchase of Blackacre *both* that Tom at some point told Ben that Blackacre was or would be held on trust for him in some proportion, *and* that Ben – by contributing to the purchase of Blackacre – acted to his detriment in that belief.

The effect of Lord Diplock's words have been to set courts and academics alike on a 50-year wild goose chase, trying to nail down when we can infer from Ben's actions that he was told by Tom that Blackacre would be held on trust for him, and to what extent, and what remedy should be available to Ben where he was so told. Textbooks will witness to the havoc that has been wrought on the law as a result; there is no need (and no space) to tell the story here. It took the English courts almost 90 years to free themselves of the effect of another monomaniac's suggestion that there must be *one* test or formula that would tell us in any given situation whether a defendant owed a claimant a duty of care (*Donoghue* v *Stevenson* [1932] AC 562, 580 (per Lord Atkin)), so if history is any guide Lord Diplock's baleful influence on this area of the law still has some way to run.

UNAUTHORISED GAINS MADE BY A FIDUCIARY

Fay will be a fiduciary for Pat if (i) Fay performs certain functions for Pat *and* (ii) the law will prevent Fay from making a gain for herself (that Pat did not authorise Fay to make for herself) if Fay's making that gain might impair Fay's properly performing those functions for Pat.

A trustee is a prime example of a fiduciary: as we saw in chapter one, in *Keech* v *Sandford* (1726) Sel Cas T King 61, the trustee in that case was prevented from renewing a lease for his own benefit when he originally held that lease on trust for an infant. But not all fiduciaries are trustees. As we also saw in chapter one, from *Boardman* v *Phipps* [1967] 2 AC 46, solicitors are fiduciaries for their clients. Other functionaries who are fiduciaries are: agents for their principals (*De Bussche* v *Alt* (1878) 8 Ch D 286), directors for their companies (*Parker* v *McKenna* (1874) LR 10 Ch App 96), partners for their fellow partners (*Aas* v *Benham* [1891] 2 Ch 244), certain joint venturers for their co-venturers (*Murad* v *Al-Saraj* [2005] EWCA Civ 959), and public officials for the government (*Reading* v *Attorney-General* [1951] AC 507). An employee is a fiduciary for his employer to the extent that they are not allowed to accept a bribe to get them to breach their contract of employment, but they are not otherwise a fiduciary (*University of Nottingham* v *Fishel* [2000] ICR 1462, 1490–91).

After some hesitations (*Lister* v *Stubbs* (1890) 45 Ch D 1; *Sinclair Investments (UK) Ltd* v *Versailles Trade Finance Ltd* [2012] Ch 453), the

UK Supreme Court has firmly ruled that if Fay is a fiduciary for Pat and makes a gain in circumstances where she is liable to account to Pat for the value of that gain, then she will also hold that gain on a constructive trust for Pat: *FHR European Ventures LLP* v *Cedar Capital Partners LLC* [2015] AC 250. The ruling has the merit of simplicity, but as the UK Supreme Court itself admitted (at [32]), there are no convincing arguments of principle why a constructive trust should arise in this situation.

It was said in a previous case that the trust arises because 'Equity treats as done what ought to be done' and therefore regards Fay as already having handed over her unauthorised gain to Pat: *Attorney-General for Hong Kong* v *Reid* [1994] 1 AC 324, 331 (per Lord Templeman) (see also Millett 2012, 591–93). However, if Fay's only duty is to account to Pat for the *value* of the gain that she has made, finding that Fay holds that gain on constructive trust for Pat gives Pat more than Fay was duty-bound to give him: he gets the very gain that Fay made, and not just the value of it. Test it this way. Suppose that Fay is Pat's agent, and Fay accepts a bribe of £5,000 in cash from Pat's business rival to allow the rival a clear field in bidding for a particular item that Fay was supposed to try to secure for Pat. Back in her hotel room, Fay feels guilty about accepting the bribe, and makes an electronic transfer of £5,000 from her bank account into Pat's account. Has Fay done everything she was supposed to do by way of accounting for the bribe she received? If so, then finding that she holds the bank notes with which he was bribed on trust for Pat is *de trop* – Fay was only supposed to account to Pat for the value of the bribe, not the very bribe itself.

Probably the best reason for finding that an unauthorised gain made by a fiduciary is held on constructive trust is that doing so forces the fiduciary not only to disgorge the gain that they have made, but also anything they have acquired using that gain. This was the case in *Reid*, where the defendant in that case was a public prosecutor who accepted bribes to obstruct certain people from being prosecuted. He then invested the bribes in buying houses. Finding the bribes were held on constructive trust for the government meant the houses he had bought with the bribes were also held on trust. Merely allowing the government a personal action against the defendant for the full value of the gains he made from his bribe-taking (as favoured by Goode 2018, 340–43) would not be as effective a means of ensuring that the bribe-taker cannot hope to benefit in any way from taking the bribe.

4. TRUSTS ARISING ON TRUST FAILURE

It is always open to a settlor to provide what should happen if the trusts that he seeks to create can no longer be performed as he intended. But if a settlor does not so provide, the law will usually impose new trusts over the trust property. (The major exception is where Sal transfers property to Tom to hold on trust for Ben and after the trust is validly constituted, Ben dies. Unless Sal has specified otherwise, Tom will simply hold on trust for Ben's heirs and the trust will continue.) These new trusts will normally involve the trustee's holding the trust assets on trust for the settlor (or the settlor's estate). However, different rules apply where the trust created by the settlor was charitable in nature. For example, if the trust was initially validly constituted but can now no longer be performed, no resulting trust back to the settlor will arise. Instead, under the law on *cy-près*, the assets of the trust will be held on new charitable trusts similar to the old ones that failed.

RESULTING TRUSTS

Where Sal has transferred assets to Tom to hold on a trust that is not charitable in nature, Tom will normally hold those assets on a resulting trust for Sal if (i) the trust fails *ab initio* (because it was never valid or could never be performed) or (ii) the trust was (very unusually) a valid non-charitable purpose trust that was validly created but a change of circumstances meant the purpose of the trust cannot now be fulfilled. Tom will only *normally* hold on resulting trust for Sal if (i) or (ii) are true because if Sal has provided what should happen in such a situation, then Sal's wishes will prevail (if they can be given effect to) and a resulting trust will *not* arise. So while the resulting trusts that arise when (i) or (ii) happens are often called 'automatic', this is a misnomer: *Westdeutsche Landesbank v Islington LBC* [1996] AC 669, 708 (per Lord Browne-Wilkinson). They will normally arise in these situations, but not automatically.

As to *why* Tom will hold on resulting trust for Sal when (i) or (ii) is the case, this is a bit of a mystery, with William Swadling going so far as to say that the question 'defies legal analysis' (Swadling 2008, 102). Unlike the (presumed) resulting trust that arises when Sal gratuitously transfers land to Tom, we cannot say that the resulting trust that arises on trust failure is an intended trust. This is because of *Vandervell* v *Inland Revenue Commissioners* [1967] AC 291. Recall (p 64) that when Vandervell instructed his trustees to transfer 100,000 shares to the Royal College of Surgeons ('RCS'), he also told them to retain an option to repurchase the shares. Vandervell clearly intended that the trustees should hold that option to repurchase on trust, but he did not specify for whom. But equally clearly, Vandervell did not intend that the option to repurchase should be held on trust for *him*, as that would have made him liable for tax on the dividends paid on the RCS's shares. Despite this, the House of Lords found that the option to repurchase was held on trust for him.

It is this that led Megarry J in the sequel to *Vandervell* – *Re Vandervell's Trusts (No 2)* [1974] Ch 269 – to suggest (at 289) that resulting trusts arising from trust failure were 'automatic', arising independently of the settlor's intention. Megarry J endorsed Lord Upjohn's suggestion in *Vandervell* (at 313) that such trusts arose because the settlor had failed to dispose of his 'beneficial interest' in the trust assets. But such a theory is contradicted by the other half of *Vandervell*, which held that when a beneficiary under a trust instructs the trustee to transfer the trust assets to a third party so that they become the beneficial owner of them, the beneficiary is not disposing of whatever interest they have under the trust to the third party, but destroying their interest. The beneficial owner has *nothing* of what the beneficiary under a trust has. It follows that where Sal settles assets on Tom on a trust that fails with the result that Tom holds on trust for Sal, Sal has rights over those assets that she never had when she was the beneficial owner of those assets. The existence of those rights cannot therefore be explained on the basis that Sal did not effectively dispose of those rights to someone else.

It has been argued that Sal's rights arise in order to prevent Tom's being unjustly enriched at Sal's expense (Birks 1992, Chambers 1997) – the idea being that where Sal settles assets on Tom on a trust that fails, then unless the law intervenes and imposes a trust over those assets for Sal's benefit, Tom will be free to walk off with the assets when Sal never intended that Tom should benefit from those assets. But it is not necessary to impose a trust here to prevent unjust enrichment (see Swadling 2008, 101) – allowing Sal to sue Tom for the value of the assets he received from her would be enough. However, a more fundamental objection to this explanation takes us to the probable right answer as to why a resulting trust arises on trust failure.

The more fundamental objection is that Tom could never be free to walk away with the trust assets. Recall (p 4) that Tom's title to the trust assets derives from his occupying the office of trustee. Tom cannot hold those assets in any other way. So Tom *must* hold on trust for someone, and the only person Tom can hold on trust for – given that the original trusts on which Tom was supposed to hold have failed – is Sal. Maitland got it right (as he so often did): 'I devise land unto and to the use of A and his heirs upon certain trusts. These trusts fail in my lifetime ... I have made A a trustee for somebody, and a trustee he must be – if for no one else then for me or my representatives' (Maitland 1936, 77; see also Mee 2017, 221–23, where this quote from Maitland appears). If this is correct, then when a resulting trust arises in response to trust failure, that trust is not only imposed but (to borrow a phrase from the film *The Matrix* (1999)) *inevitable*.

CY-PRÈS

When discussing what happens when a charitable trust fails, a number of different situations need to be distinguished. (For the history of the law in this area, see Jones 1969, 72–89, 138–53; Mitchell 2020.)

First, where Sal transfers assets to Tom to hold on a trust that Sal *intends* to be charitable but is not (because it is not for a charitable purpose, or does not satisfy the public benefit requirement, or was not *exclusively* charitable but had some non-charitable purposes mixed into it) and is therefore invalid, then Tom will hold those assets on a resulting trust for Sal, unless Sal has specified what should happen in the event of the trust's being invalid. This is what happened in *Re Diplock* [1951] AC 251, where the brewer Caleb Diplock left £263,000 in his will, directing his executors to use the money for whatever 'charitable or benevolent ... objects' they saw fit. The inclusion of the words 'or benevolent' invalidated the trust as some purposes may be benevolent without being charitable, with the result that the trust was not exclusively charitable. The executors therefore held that money on trust for Diplock's estate – but being unaware of this, they paid the money out to various institutions, including for the construction of a 'Caleb Diplock Ward' at Guy's Hospital.

Second, where Sal transfers assets to Tom to hold on a valid charitable trust but the trust fails *ab initio* because its purpose cannot be performed, then Tom will hold those assets on a resulting trust for Sal, unless there is evidence that Sal had a 'general charitable intention' that means Sal would have been happy for those assets to be applied for a similar charitable purpose. If there is such evidence, the trust assets will be applied for that purpose under the law on *cy-près* (where '*cy-près*' is old French for 'so close' – so assets that are applied *cy-près* are applied in a way that is 'so close' to the settlor's original intention). So if Sal left money in her will to Tom specifying that the money should be applied for the benefit of a local dogs home which had closed down by the time Sal died, it is possible that Sal would have been happy for the money to be applied for looking after abandoned dogs generally. The courts have developed various presumptions to determine whether Sal had such a 'general charitable intent' or intended that the money *only* be used for the benefit of the dogs home that she specified in her will. For example, if Sal left money in her will to Tom to be used for the benefit of a named dogs home that never actually existed, it is highly likely that Sal would have been happy for her money to be used to look after stray dogs generally, as Sal could not have formed a specific attachment to a dogs home that never existed in the first place. So in this kind of case, the law on *cy-près* will apply to impose new trusts on Tom, to use the money for the benefit of some other dogs home (*Re Harwood* [1936] 1 Ch 285).

Third, where Sal transfers assets to Tom to hold on a charitable trust that is initially validly constituted but, due to a change of circumstances, cannot subsequently be performed, then – unless Sal has specified otherwise – new trusts will be imposed over the remaining assets in the trust, requiring those assets to be applied for another charitable purpose similar to that which Sal had in mind when setting up the trust in the first place. For example, in 1928 a fund was set up with the object of its being invested so it would grow to such an amount that it could then be used to pay off the National Debt. By 2021, the fund was worth £600 million; and the National Debt was a terrifying £2.27 trillion. It was therefore impossible for the fund to be used to *discharge* the National Debt, and in *Attorney General* v *Zedra Fiduciary Services (UK) Ltd* [2022] EWHC 102 (Ch), it was held that the fund should be applied *cy-près* to *reduce* the National Debt. It used to be a rule that 'once a charitable trust has been validly created, the trust funds had to be applied to the trust's purposes for as long as this was practically possible' (Mitchell 2020, 35). However, statute has made inroads on that rule, allowing the trustees of a charitable

trust to make an application under the law on *cy-près* to change the purposes for which the trust assets are to be used where the original purposes
have ceased 'to provide a suitable and effective method of using' the trust
assets (Charities Act 2011, s 62(1)(e)(iii)) having regard to the 'spirit of
the gift' and current 'social and economic circumstances' (Charities Act
2011, s 62(2)).

4

Trustees and Third Parties

1. TYPES OF TRUSTEE

It is possible, and indeed conventional, to define a trustee as 'someone who holds assets on trust for another'. However, we have adopted – and will continue to adopt – a narrower definition, under which a trustee is 'someone who occupies the office of a trustee, and in that capacity holds assets on trust for another'.

Someone occupies the office of a trustee if either they have agreed to be a trustee, or they have knowingly meddled with trust assets that have come into their hands in such a way that it is fair to treat them as though they have agreed to be a trustee. In the first case, the trustee is known as an 'express trustee'. In the second, the trustee is known as a 'constructive trustee' – where 'constructive' means 'imposed', not 'fictional'. Not fictional because they *are* a trustee – their meddling with trust assets makes it fair to thrust upon them the responsibilities involved in being a trustee. Another name for this second kind of trustee is 'a trustee *de son tort*' ('a trustee by his wrong' in meddling with trust assets without the authority to do so). However, it should be noted that not all constructive trustees are the same. There are people who are said to be held liable for a breach of trust 'as a constructive trustee' where 'constructive' means 'fictional', not 'imposed'. That is, they are held liable for a breach of trust not because they were a trustee, but because they are treated *as though they were* a trustee.

The majority of this chapter will focus on express trustees and their duties; at the end of the chapter we will try to pick our way through the mélange of confusions that surround the law on when someone who is not an express trustee will be held liable as a result of someone's committing a breach of trust.

2. EXPRESS TRUSTEES

A trustee (to save words, in this section we will simply refer to express trustees as 'trustees') will have many duties under the trust of which they are a trustee; what those duties are will depend on what kind of trust that is. In this section, we will focus on six principal duties to which a trustee of a fixed trust will typically be subject. Three preliminary points should be made before we dive into the details.

First: '*a* trustee'. Our focus is on an individual trustee's duties because a trustee can only be held liable for breaching their own duties. As a result, they will not, without more, be held liable for another co-trustee's breach of *their* duties: *Townley* v *Sherborne* (1633) Bridg 35.

Second: 'a *fixed* trust'. Just because the focus below is on the duties typically owed by a trustee under a fixed trust does not mean that those same duties do not also apply to a trustee under a discretionary trust or a trust for purposes. They usually will, but how they do has to take into account the nature of the discretionary trust or trust for purposes in question. For example, it would make no sense to talk about the trustee of a discretionary trust, under which they are required to make a one-off distribution of assets, having a duty to invest the trust assets carefully; or a trustee of a charitable trust having a duty to act honestly in the best interests of the beneficiaries of the trust (as there are no beneficiaries).

Third: '*typically*'. With exceptions, that will be noted below, the duties below can be excluded or modified by the trust instrument setting up the trust of which the trustee is trustee.

THE CORE DUTY

The first duty of a trustee is to do what the trustee honestly thinks is in the best interests of the beneficiaries under the trust. This duty may be called the 'core duty' because it is part of the 'irreducible core' of a trust. The courts will not allow this duty to be excluded under the trust instrument setting up the trust as without this duty, there is no trust at all: *Armitage* v *Nurse* [1998] Ch 241.

Some would call this core duty the 'fiduciary duty', as they argue that the defining characteristic of a fiduciary is that they have a duty to do what they honestly think is in the best interests of the person for whom they are a fiduciary (Finn 1977, 15; Smith 2014). However, I would prefer to refer to a quite different duty – a trustee's duty not to put themselves in a position where their self-interest may conflict with their performing their duties as a trustee – as the fiduciary duty, and will do so below. Those who are attached to the idea that the core duty of a trustee is a fiduciary duty can refer to that duty as the *prescriptive* fiduciary duty ('prescriptive' meaning telling someone to do something positive) and the fiduciary duty discussed below as the *proscriptive* fiduciary duty ('proscriptive' meaning telling someone *not* to do something).

While this duty is the core duty of a trustee, it is subordinate to the other duties listed below. A trustee is required to do what they honestly think is in the best interests of their beneficiaries, but only within the boundaries imposed on them by these other duties. So a trustee cannot justify or excuse the breach of one of these other duties by claiming 'I honestly thought it was in my beneficiaries' best interests!'.

THE *VIRES* DUTY

One of the most important limits on what the trustee is permitted to do under the trust is set by what we could call 'the *vires* duty' – the duty not to do something that the trustee is not authorised to do under the trust. So if the trustee has no power to act in a particular way under the trust, they will automatically commit a breach of trust if they act in that way. Liability for breach of this kind of duty is therefore *strict* – it is no defence for a trustee to say that they honestly or reasonably thought that they had the power to do *x* when they were not authorised to do *x* under the trust: *Webb* v *Jonas* (1888) 39 Ch D 660, 665–66 (per Kekewich J).

Having said that, s 61 of the Trustee Act 1925 gives the courts a discretion to relieve a trustee of liability for committing a breach of the *vires* duty where the trustee acted 'honestly and reasonably' and could be excused 'for omitting to obtain the directions of the court in the matter in which he committed such breach'. And much of the force of the *vires* duty has been dissipated by s 3 of the Trustee Act 2000 which provides that unless the trust instrument says otherwise (s 6) 'a trustee may make any kind of investment that he could make if he were absolutely entitled to the assets of the trust'.

The *vires* duty is non-excludable but only in an uninteresting way. If the trust instrument provides that a trustee is only empowered to invest trust assets in shares or land, but also provides that the trustee cannot be sued if they invest in anything else, then the trust instrument has effectively empowered the trustee to invest in anything they like. The result is that the *vires* duty is not excluded but instead cannot be breached when it comes to the trustee's investment decisions.

THE INVESTMENT DUTY

Of course, the fact that a trustee may have a general power of investment of the type conferred by s 3 of the 2000 Act does not mean that the trustee is able to invest trust assets in anything they like. Under s 1 of the 2000 Act (read with s 2 and Schedule 1), a trustee exercising their general power of investment is required to 'exercise such skill and care as is reasonable in the circumstances' given 'any special knowledge or expertise that [they hold themselves] out as having' and – if they act 'as a trustee in the course of a business or profession' – 'any special knowledge or experience that it is reasonable to expect of a person acting in the course of that kind of business or profession.'

This provision replaces the duty of care trustees were subject to under a line of cases beginning with *Speight* v *Gaunt* (1883) 9 App Cas 1, and expressed in canonical form by Lindley LJ in *Re Whiteley* (1886) 33 Ch D 347, 355: 'The duty of a trustee is not take such care only as a prudent man would take if he had only himself to consider; the duty rather is to take such care as an ordinary prudent man would take if he were minded to make an investment for the benefit of other people for whom he felt morally bound to provide.'

The Trustee Act 2000 makes clear that the investment duty may be limited or excluded by the trust instrument (Schedule 1, Paragraph 7), and in other trust jurisdictions it has been accepted that what has become known as an 'anti-*Bartlett* clause', excluding the trustee's duty of care in respect both to making investment decisions and monitoring investments once made, will be valid: *Zhang Hong Li* v *DBS Bank (Hong Kong) Ltd* [2019] HKCFA 45, [65]. (Such clauses are known as 'anti-*Bartlett*' clauses because another in the line of cases setting out the trustee's duty of care in respect of investments is *Bartlett* v *Barclays Bank* [1980] Ch 515, 531–32.) Moreover, it is an essential feature of a VISTA trust (p 21) that the trustee owes no such duty of care to their beneficiaries, as the trustee of such a trust over shares in a family business is required not to concern themselves with how that business is doing or being run.

The trustee's duty of care in respect of investments does not, therefore, form part of the 'irreducible core' of what it means to be a trustee (for criticism, see Fee 2020).

It has been held that a trustee has to have in mind the *financial* interests of the beneficiaries in determining what they are required to do under the investment duty. So a trustee who honestly thinks that it is not in the *best interests overall* of a beneficiary to profit from an investment in a company that relies on child labour to mine cobalt for electric car and mobile phone batteries (see Amnesty International 2016) – praying in aid McBride 2019, 100–02 – had best keep their thoughts to themselves, and invest in the company in question if that would be in the beneficiary's best interests *financially*: *Cowan* v *Scargill* [1985] Ch 270. (Though it would, of course, be different if the beneficiary authorised the trustee not to invest in companies using child labour.) The same is, generally speaking, true when it comes to investing funds held on a charitable trust. The trustees are not entitled to take into account ethical considerations when investing the charity's money. The only exceptions are where *not* taking into account such considerations would either (a) result in the charity's funds being invested in a way that contradicted the purposes of the charity (such as a cancer research charity's funds being invested in a tobacco company) or (b) result in a net financial loss to the charity as a result of donors refusing to donate to the charity because it has made a particular investment: *Harries* v *Church Commissioners of England* [1992] 1 WLR 1241, 1246–47; *Butler-Sloss* v *Charity Commission* [2022] Ch 371, [78]. (The same principles would apply in the case where someone proposes to donate to a charity – the charity would be obliged to accept the donation unless considerations such as (a) or (b) applied.)

Having said that, as we will see in chapter five, it is so difficult to predict the outcome of a particular investment or investment strategy that a trustee will usually have enough wiggle room within the confines of the investment duty to adopt an 'ethical' investment policy on the grounds that they reasonably believe doing so will provide as good or better returns than one which simply focuses on maximising financial returns: Nicholls 1995; Law Commission 2014, chapter 5.

THE FIDUCIARY DUTY

As was observed in the previous chapter (p 74), a trustee is a fiduciary and as such is subject to what Lord Herschell in *Bray* v *Ford* [1896]

AC 44 described as (at 51) 'an inflexible rule of ... Equity that a person in a fiduciary position ... is not, unless otherwise expressly provided, entitled to make a profit [from their position]; he is not allowed to put himself in a position where his interest and duty conflict.' Statements such as these have led people to believe that a trustee is subject to *two* fiduciary rules – a 'no profit' rule that requires the trustee not to make a profit from their position, and a 'no conflict' rule that requires the trustee not to put themselves in a position where their self-interest may come into conflict with their properly performing one of their other duties as a trustee.

Having said that, there is no case involving a trustee (or, more generally, any fiduciary) being made to give up a gain they have obtained that cannot be explained on the basis of the 'no conflict' rule. For example, *Keech* v *Sandford* (1726) Sel Cas T King 61 is often said to provide an example of the 'no profit' rule in action, the defendant in that case having obtained the opportunity to renew the lease for his own benefit from having previously held the lease on trust for the infant claimant: see, for example, Cretney 1969, 162–63. However, it is easy enough to identify the conflict in *Keech* which the court sought to avoid by holding that the defendant trustee was not allowed to renew the lease for his own benefit. When the defendant was told that the lessor was unwilling to renew the lease if it was going to be held on trust for the claimant, the defendant – as trustee for the claimant – had to decide whether there was any point in trying to get the lessor to change his mind, and if so attempt to do so. Obviously, the trustee's ability to perform that duty properly would come into conflict with his self-interest if the trustee thought that should negotiations with the lessor on behalf of the claimant prove unfruitful, the trustee could renew the lease for his own benefit. As King LC observed in *Keech*, 'I very well see, if a trustee, on the refusal to renew, might have a lease to himself, few trust-estates would be renewed to *cestuis que use*' (62).

It is therefore doubtful whether the 'no profit' rule actually exists (for discussion, see Conaglen 2010, 113–25; Worthington 2013, 730–35). Certainly, Lord Herschell did not seem to think he was articulating two distinct rules in *Bray* v *Ford*. He went on to explain that 'the rule' (note: singular) he had set out was based on avoiding conflicts between a fiduciary's interests and their duties – 'it [is] based on the consideration that, human nature being what it is, there is danger, in such circumstances [where the rule applies], of the person holding a fiduciary position being swayed by interest rather than by duty, and thus prejudicing those whom he was bound to protect.' A trustee's fiduciary duty not to put themselves in a position where their self-interest comes into conflict with their other duties as a trustee is therefore clearly intended to help ensure that those other duties are properly performed – but how does it do this?

It is sometimes said that the fiduciary duty *deters* trustees from giving into the temptation to breach some other duty that they owe their beneficiaries in order to make a gain for themselves (see Conaglen 2010, 61–76, 80–84). However, this explanation is weakened by the fact that the fiduciary duty does not just apply to trustees who are positively tempted to put themselves before their beneficiaries. It also applies to trustees who are honestly trying to do their best for their beneficiaries, with the courts being very clear that it is *vitally* important that it apply to such non-tempted trustees, with James LJ observing in *Parker* v *McKenna* (1874) LR 10 Ch App 96 that the 'safety of mankind' (125) depended on the fiduciary duty being applied 'inexorably' (124) by the courts to *all* fiduciaries, and not just fiduciaries who might be tempted by the prospect of making a gain to do something that might prejudice the interests of the person for whom they are a fiduciary. It is also not clear how someone can be deterred from dishonestly making a gain for themselves by being required not to make it and being told that if they do make it, it can be taken away from them. Surely they would still go ahead and make the gain for themselves, on the basis that the worst that could happen is that they will merely have to give the gain up, and that this is not guaranteed to happen. (Compare a university telling students that if they are caught cheating on an exam, all that will happen to them is that they will have to resit the exam – no student would be deterred from cheating by such a rule.)

We come closer to the mark when we realise (as did, independently, Samet 2008, McBride 2013, Smith 2014) that it is a sad fact of human nature that people can *fool themselves* into thinking that they are doing the right thing by acting in a particular way when what is actually motivating them to act in that way – and to think that they are doing the right thing thereby – is the gain they stand to make for themselves by acting in that way. (An excellent real-life example of this process at work is provided by the film *Inside Job* (2010), scrutinising the failure of academic economists to predict the 2008 economic crisis.) It is to free trustees of the distorting effect that the prospect of making a gain will have on their judgment that they come under a duty not to make a gain from acting in a way that might result in their breaching a duty owed to their beneficiaries.

For example, in *Keech* v *Sandford* if the trustee were permitted to take the lease for his own benefit if it could not be renewed for the benefit of the claimant, it is entirely predictable that the trustee would conclude that there was no chance of the lessor being persuaded to renew the lease for the benefit of the claimant when there was a possibility that he could have been so persuaded. In order to ensure that the trustee – who is assumed to be honest, but is also human and therefore capable of fooling himself about the lessor's negotiating stance – remained as clear-sighted as possible about the prospects of renewing the lease for the benefit of the claimant, the law imposed on him a duty not to take the lease for his own benefit. As King LC observed (at 62), 'This may seem hard, that the trustee is the only person of all mankind who might not have the lease: but it is very proper that rule should be strictly pursued, and not in the least relaxed; for it is very obvious what would be the consequence of letting trustees have the lease, on refusal to renew to *cestui que use*.'

The trustee's fiduciary duty can be relaxed or excluded altogether either by the trust instrument or the (fully informed) consent of the beneficiaries. So the professionalisation and commercialisation of trusteeship means that it is routine for trustees to be paid for the job they do administering the trust (see Langbein 2005, 939–41, 976–78) and when it comes to investing the trust assets, the trust instrument can specify that the trustee will be paid according to results – in other words, their fees will be performance-related. This is so even though performance-related pay ('PRP') can create exactly the kind of distorting effect that the fiduciary duty is intended to free trustees of, making trustees underestimate the risks attached to investments or commitments that promise high rewards for the trust fund and therefore the trustee: see Noe and Young 2014. It was the prevalence of PRP among key players in American banks and associated institutions that was responsible for those players making on behalf of their employers what were for them very lucrative investments and commitments that they consequently fooled themselves into thinking were completely safe. In fact, those investments and commitments built the 'doomsday machine' (Lewis 2011) that exploded in 2008, making those deluded players' employers effectively insolvent and almost destroying the world economy; and the doomsday machine they built may still prove to have doomed the world's long-term economic viability. Just as James LJ predicted 134 years before, in *Parker* v *McKenna*, a weakening of the fiduciary duty resulted in the 'safety of mankind' being endangered: see, further, Getzler 2014.

THE DUTY TO ACCOUNT

The fiduciary duty is one means by which Equity seeks to ensure that a trustee performs their other duties. The duty to account is (or perhaps was) another. The duty to account requires a trustee to account for their management of the trust and put the trust fund in the position that it would have been if it had been properly managed.

Both outgoings from, and incomings to, the trust fund are scrutinised under the accounting process. If the beneficiaries under the trust successfully allege that a particular disbursement of trust assets was improper, then that disbursement is said to be *falsified* and the trustee is required to restore the value of the disbursed assets to the trust fund. If the beneficiaries successfully allege that the trustee has not added to the trust fund assets that they ought to have added, then the trust fund is said to be *surcharged* and the trustee is required to add to the trust fund the value of the missing assets. (The literature on this process is now enormous, but particularly valuable resources are Chambers 2002, 16–20; Meagher, Gummow and Lehane 2014, ch 26; Watson 2016, ch 5; Ho 2016, 851–60; Elliott 2020, ch 20, §2.)

As Lord Millett and others (see Edelman and Elliott 2004, 118; Getzler 2011, 978–79; Mitchell 2014, 221–24) have emphasised, the duty to account does not arise as a remedy for a breach of trust but is rather a means of ensuring that a trustee performs his duties under the trust: 'an account is not a remedy for [a] wrong. Trustees … are accounting parties, and their beneficiaries … do not have to prove that there has been a breach of trust … in order to obtain an order for account. Once the trust … is established or conceded the beneficiary … is entitled to an account as of right. Although like all equitable remedies an order for an account is discretionary, in making the order the court is not granting a remedy for [a] wrong but enforcing performance of an obligation' (*Libertarian Investments Ltd* v *Hall* [2013] HKCFA 93, [167] (per Lord Millett NPJ); see also Millett 2008, 225).

A couple of examples can be provided of the duty to account at work. In *Cocker* v *Quayle* (1830) 1 Russ & M 535, money was held on trust for a wife for life with the power to lend money from the trust fund to her husband, provided the wife consented and the husband provided a bond, guaranteeing that the trust fund would be repaid the lent money. The trustees loaned the husband money with the wife's consent, but without obtaining a bond from him. The husband then went bankrupt in circumstances that meant the bond would have been useless to recover the money loaned to the husband. It was held that the 'trust fund ... must be replaced' by the trustees (538). The trustees had no authority to lend money to the husband in the way that they did: the fact that there might have been some other way they could have validly loaned money to the husband (and lost it on his bankruptcy) was immaterial.

In *Kellaway* v *Johnson* (1842) 5 Beav 319, trustees held bonds that would pay out £3,000 when they came due on trust for the claimant. The trustees improperly sold the bonds. Lord Langdale MR required the trustees to restore to the trust fund bonds of equivalent value to those they had sold. The result was endorsed by Street J in *Re Dawson* [1966] 2 NSWR 211, observing that 'the obligation to make restitution, which courts of equity have from very early times imposed on defaulting trustees and other fiduciaries is of a more absolute nature than the common law obligation to pay damages for [a] tort or breach of contract' (216). He went on to hold that 'The obligation to restore to the estate the assets of which [a trustee] deprived it necessarily connotes that, where a monetary compensation is to be paid in lieu of restoring assets, that compensation is to be assessed by reference to the value of the assets at the date of restoration and not at the date of deprivation. In that sense the obligation is a continuing one and ... will fall for quantification at the date when recoupment is to be effected, and not before' (ibid).

THE DUTY TO COMPENSATE

As a method for keeping trustees on the straight and narrow, the duty to account has arguably now been displaced by a duty to compensate the beneficiaries of a trust for losses resulting from the trustee's breach of trust. The House of Lords' decision in *Target Holdings Ltd* v *Redferns* [1996] AC 421 provided the first suggestion that the English courts might be moving away from the accounting process and towards awards of equitable compensation as the primary vehicle for disciplining trustees when it came to performance of their non-fiduciary duties.

In *Target Holdings*, Target agreed to lend Crowngate £1.5 million to acquire some commercial property in Birmingham; the loan to be secured by a mortgage over the land (which Target thought was worth the £2 million Crowngate was paying for it). The loan money was advanced to Redferns, a firm of solicitors that was acting for both Target and Crowngate, and was held on a bare trust for Target with instructions to pay the money over to the sellers of the property once the property had been conveyed into Crowngate's name. Redferns jumped too soon in advancing the money, paying it out between 29 June and 3 July 1991, when Crowngate only acquired the property and Target obtained a charge over it on 5 July. Crowngate was subsequently wound up as insolvent in September 1991 and Target tried to recover the money it had loaned Crowngate by selling the property over which it had a mortgage. It was at that point Target realised the commercial property purchased by Crowngate was not worth anywhere near the £2 million Crowngate had paid for it, and they could only recover £500,000 on selling it, leaving them with a £1 million loss on the transaction.

Target sued Redferns, arguing that Redferns had acted improperly in paying out early the purchase money that Target had advanced to Redferns and which Redferns had held on trust for Target. On an accounting approach to Redferns' liability, it might have been thought that Target would succeed: Redferns paid out money held on trust for Target improperly and as a result would have to restore that money. However, Lord Browne-Wilkinson – giving the only judgment – treated the case from the very beginning as one where Target was suing Redferns for equitable compensation for the loss that it had suffered as a result of a breach of trust. He observed that the case raised 'a novel point', which was 'Is [a trustee who commits a breach of trust] liable to compensate the beneficiary not only for losses caused by the breach but also for losses which the beneficiary would, in any event, have suffered even if there had been no such breach?' (428). The fact that this was regarded as a 'novel point' in 1996 is an indication of just how novel the House of Lords' approach to determining Redferns' liability was. But framed as it was, the point could only have one answer – obviously a trustee who committed a breach of trust could *not* be held liable to pay compensation for a loss that would have been suffered regardless of that breach of trust being committed. As a result, Redferns owed Target nothing: had it not jumped the gun and paid out the purchase money when it was supposed to, Target would have suffered exactly the same loss.

It was possible to argue that the House of Lords' decision in *Target* was 'muddled' (Mitchell 2013, 323) or that it was 'very difficult to know' (Birks 1996, 47) whether the House of Lords meant to revolutionise the approach adopted to determine the liability of errant trustees. However, the same could not be said of *Target*'s sequel, which was the UK Supreme Court's decision in *AIB Group (UK) plc v Mark Redler & Co* [2015] AC 1503. By then, the arguments that *Target* had (perhaps unintentionally) changed the law's approach to errant trustees – no longer requiring them to live up to their primary obligations through the accounting process, but instead requiring them to compensate beneficiaries for the losses suffered by them as a result of their breach of trust – were widely known. In the face of those arguments, the UK Supreme Court affirmed *Target* and held that the defendant trustees in *AIB* should only be held liable to compensate the claimant beneficiary for the losses suffered by it as a result of the defendants' breach of trust.

AIB was another case involving a bank lending money on property that turned out to be an inadequate security for the loan. In 2006, Mr and Mrs Sondhi wanted to remortgage their home which was valued as being worth £4.25 million. At the time Barclays had a mortgage over the Sondhis' home, securing a loan of £1.5 million to the couple. The Sondhis wanted AIB to lend them £3.3 million, which AIB was willing to do, so long as £1.5 million of that £3.3 million was used to pay off the Barclays loan, so that AIB would then have a first charge over the Sondhis' home. Redler was the firm of solicitors used by AIB to effect the loan to the Sondhis. AIB advanced £3.3 million to Redler: Redler held the money on a bare trust for AIB and was instructed to use the money first to pay off the Barclays loan and then give the rest to the Sondhis. Unfortunately, Redler thought that the Sondhis only owed Barclays £1.2 million, not £1.5 million. So it paid Barclays £1.2 million and paid the rest to the Sondhis. The result was that Barclays still had a mortgage over the Sondhis' house for £300,000, and AIB had to settle – once Redler's mistake came to light – for a second charge over the house to secure its loan to the Sondhis of £3.3 million. So long as the house was still worth £4.25 million, AIB was still protected – but come the economic crisis in 2008, the price of the house plummeted and the Sondhis were unable to keep repaying the money they owed AIB and Barclays. The house was sold for £1.2 million, of which Barclays got to keep the first £300,000; AIB therefore only recovered £900,000 of their £3.3 million loan.

AIB sued Redler on the basis that it had acted improperly in disbursing the £3.3 million that it held on trust for AIB without getting a first charge over the Sondhis' house in return. The UK Supreme Court readily found that Redler had committed a breach of trust in acting as they did – but went on to hold that AIB was limited to suing Redler for equitable compensation for the loss that it had suffered as a result of Redler's breach of trust. This loss came to £300,000: the extra amount of money AIB would have obtained on the sale of the Sondhis' house had Redler done what it was supposed to and paid off the Barclays loan in full, allowing AIB a first charge over the house.

Lord Millett argued that the decision in *AIB* was right in the result, but 'heretical' in its reasoning, arguing that equitable compensation can only ever be awarded where a traditional, specific, equitable remedy – such as rescission, or specific performance, or an account – is unavailable, and that was not the case in *AIB* (Millett 2015, 202–05). Lusina Ho and Richard Nolan have similarly argued that the result in *AIB* could have been reached under traditional accounting principles (Ho and Nolan 2020, 414–15). However, it has to be accepted in light of *AIB* that the duty to compensate is – rightly or wrongly – now recognised as a duty that a trustee who has committed a breach of trust is subject to, and it is now quite urgent that we find some answers to the following questions that the recognition of that duty has given rise to.

(1) *Relationship with account.* It is not clear that the recognition of the duty to compensate has consigned the duty to account to history.

In *Target*, Lord Browne-Wilkinson suggested three cases where the duty to account would remain the principal vehicle for disciplining an errant trustee: (a) where the trust was a commercial trust created for the purposes of effecting a transaction that had not yet been completed (436); (b) where the trust is a traditional, domestic trust that is still subsisting (434); and (c) where the breach of trust is fraudulent (432).

In *AIB*, the UK Supreme Court indicated that it agreed with the traditional accounting approach being adopted in (a) ([74], per Lord Toulson; [90], per Lord Reed), but it took the view that the transaction in *AIB* had been effectively completed, despite AIB's not getting what it bargained for ([74], per Lord Toulson). Lord Toulson expressed some support for the accounting approach being adopted in both (b) ([67], [70]) and (c) ([62]). Lord Reed did not deal with fraudulent breaches of trust, and so far as (b) was concerned, Lord Reed took the view that it would be wrong to say that there was 'a categorical distinction between trusts in commercial and non-commercial relationships', but rather 'the duties and liabilities of trustees may depend, in some respects, on the terms of the trust ... and the relationship between the relevant parties' ([102]).

Alexis Georgiou has interestingly suggested that a beneficiary should only be entitled to seek to hold a trustee to account for their management of the trust fund where they have a 'legitimate interest' in doing so. In all other cases, they should be confined to suing for equitable compensation for losses that they have suffered as a result of the trustee's breach of trust: Georgiou 2021. (For the role that the concept of a 'legitimate interest' plays in contract law, see McBride 2017, 55–59.) The fact that such a suggestion can be made nowadays – and in England's premier law journal – shows how very far trusts law has travelled from the days, not so long ago, when it was said that 'accountability is the backbone of the trustee's liability, and all breaches of trust have to be analysed on that basis' (Birks 1996, 46).

(2) *Picking the right counterfactual.* Determining whether a trustee's breach of trust caused the trust fund or the trust's beneficiaries loss requires one to imagine what the world would have been liked had that breach of trust not occurred. To do that can involve a very close analysis of what the trustee was actually required to do, as the case of *Various Claimants* v *Giambrone & Law* [2017] EWCA Civ 1193 shows.

In that case, the defendants were a firm of solicitors representing various individuals – the claimants in this case – who wanted to buy 'off plan' apartments that were being constructed on a particular site in Calabria, Italy. Every time the defendants paid over the claimants' deposits to secure an apartment, the defendants were supposed to ensure that there was a guarantee in place issued by a bank or some other body under which the claimants would be repaid their deposits if the developers became insolvent. Unfortunately, the defendants never did this, and therefore committed a breach of trust when they paid over the claimants' deposits to the developers. The development ran into trouble when it was alleged that it was bound up with a money laundering scheme operated by the Mafia and the IRA, and the apartments were never built. However, the developers never became insolvent, so even if the guarantees that were meant to protect the claimants' deposits had been issued, they would not have helped the claimants get their money back.

The claimants sued the defendants for equitable compensation for the loss they claimed to have suffered as a result of the defendants' breach of trust. The defendants argued no loss had been suffered – they would not have committed a breach of trust had they paid over the claimants' deposits having first obtained a guarantee to protect them, and had they done that the claimants would still be as badly off as they were today. The Court of Appeal rejected this argument, holding that the defendants' duty was not an *active* duty to pay over the deposits and get a guarantee in return, but a *passive* duty to hold on to the deposits until guarantees were issued to protect those deposits. Had the defendants complied with that passive duty, then the defendants would still be holding the claimants' deposits on trust for them, and the claimants could recover those deposits back.

One way in which a trustee can avoid committing a breach of trust is to obtain the consent of the beneficiaries to whatever it is the trustee is proposing to do. Is it open to a trustee who has committed a breach of trust by doing x to argue that 'The fact that I committed a *breach of trust* by doing x caused the trust fund/beneficiaries no loss because had I asked the beneficiaries, they would have consented to my doing x and so I could have done x without committing a breach of trust'?

It is not open to a trustee to make an argument like that in a fiduciary duty case. Where they have made a gain from doing x and doing x might have involved their committing a breach of trust, they cannot retain the gain on the basis that had they asked the beneficiaries, the beneficiaries would have consented to their making that gain: *Murad* v *Al-Saraj* [2005] EWCA Civ 959, [71] (per Arden LJ), [100] (per Parker LJ) (though see Clarke LJ's more flexible approach at [141]).

It used to be thought that the same would be true in a claim for equitable compensation. A trustee who committed a breach of trust by entering into an improvident transaction and thereby caused loss to the trust fund/beneficiaries could *not* escape liability for that loss by saying 'But had I asked the beneficiaries they would have consented to my entering into that transaction!': *Brickenden* v *London Loan & Saving Co* [1934] 3 DLR 465, 469 (per Lord Thankerton). However, the law in this area must now be regarded as unsettled, with the Court of Appeal holding in *Auden McKenzie* v *Patel* [2019] EWCA Civ 2291 that it was *arguable* that a company director who was being sued for equitable compensation in respect of payments that he unlawfully had the company make to companies controlled by him and his sister would not be held liable if he could prove that had he not done this, he would have lawfully paid out the same amount of money to him and his sister as premiums on their shareholdings in the company. In *Swindle* v *Harrison* [1997] 4 All ER 705, Evans LJ went further and held that a trustee would *not* normally be held liable to pay equitable compensation where they could show that their beneficiaries would have consented to whatever it was that the trustee did to cause the trust fund/beneficiaries loss. He suggested (at 717) that *Brickenden* would only apply where the trustee acted fraudulently in committing the breach of trust. However, Richards LJ observed in *Auden McKenzie* (at [63]) that 'It does not seem to accord with principle that equitable compensation should be payable only because the defendant has acted dishonestly.'

(3) *Burden of proof.* Under the accounting process, the burden of proof largely fell on the defendant trustee – it was up to the trustee to show that a particular disbursement or loss to the trust fund was justified. (The exception was where the beneficiaries sought to surcharge the trust fund for some gain that they allege the trustee should have made – in such a case they would have to make out 'a case of suspicion in the mind of the Court' (Chambers 2002, 19) that this had happened before the burden fell on the trustee to clear themselves of the suspicion or pay up.) By contrast, in a claim for damages for a tort or a breach of contract, the burden of proving wrongdoing and causation of loss falls entirely on the claimant. Lusina Ho argues convincingly that at least in cases where the beneficiaries under a trust are claiming compensation in respect of a positive loss to them or the trust fund (as opposed to a failure to receive a gain), the burden of proof should remain on the trustee to show that the loss was innocently caused: 'To inspire the beneficiary's confidence in the trustee's discharge of his duty, equity should not allocate the burden of proof in such a way that requires the beneficiary to constantly check on the trustee and maintain records of the latter's dealing [with] the trust property lest there be future litigation against [them]' (Ho 2016, 872).

(4) *Application of common law rules on compensatory awards.* As against a contract breaker or a tortfeasor, compensatory damages may be awarded in respect of (a) losses (including consequential losses) that were *caused* by the breach of contract/tort, and that were (b) not too *remote* a consequence of the breach of contract/tort, and were (c) within the '*scope of the duty*' breached by the contract breaker/tortfeasor, and that (d) the victim of the breach of contract/tort could not reasonably have avoided

by *mitigating* the losses suffered by them as a result of that breach of contract/tort. Moreover, the damages payable to the contract breaker/ tortfeasor will be reduced for (e) *contributory negligence* in cases where the breach of contract/tort involved the breach of a duty of care and the claimant was partly to blame for the loss that they suffered.

It will take years for the courts to work out how much of this will also applies to claims for equitable compensation arising out of a breach of contract (for discussion of the current state of play, see Elliott 2002, Glister 2014, Davies 2018). Already there are disagreements. In *Bristol & West Building Society* v *Mothew* [1998] Ch 1, Millett LJ stated (at 17) that there is 'no reason in principle why the common law rules of causation, remoteness of damage and measure of damages should not be applied by analogy' in cases where beneficiaries seek equitable compensation in respect of a trustee's 'breach of the duty of skill and care' owed under the investment duty. By contrast, Lord Reed said in *AIB* that when it comes to equitable compensation the 'foreseeability of loss is generally irrelevant' ([135]) while the loss being compensated must 'flow directly from' the trustee's breach of trust so that 'Losses resulting from unreasonable behaviour on the part of the claimant will be adjudged to flow from that behaviour, and not from the breach' (ibid) – when none of those propositions are true of a defendant's liability to pay damages in contract or tort.

3. THIRD PARTY LIABILITIES

OVERVIEW

We can summarise the law in this area by supposing that Tom holds a painting on trust for Ben and Cat, and in breach of trust Tom transfers that painting to Vic, a volunteer:

(1) *Proprietary claims.* Vic will hold that painting on trust for Ben and Cat as he is not a *bona fide* purchaser for value without notice, with the result that Ben and Cat will be able to recover the painting from Vic under the rule in *Saunders* v *Vautier*, so long as it is still in Vic's hands. If Vic has disposed of the painting but was paid £10,000 for it and the £10,000 is still in Vic's hands, then Ben and Cat will be able to claim Vic holds that £10,000 on trust for them as it represents the traceable proceeds of assets

that were held on trust for them. They will therefore be able to recover that £10,000 from Vic under the rule in *Saunders* v *Vautier*.

(2) *The rule in Re Diplock*. If Vic innocently receives and gives away the painting, getting nothing in return for it, then Vic will not be liable to Ben and Cat unless 'the rule in *Re Diplock*' applies. (The facts of *Re Diplock* were set out above, on p 78.) This rule says that if Tom was *the executor of a will* and in that capacity misapplied a painting that he was supposed under the will to hold on trust for Ben and Cat, transferring it to Vic instead, then Vic will be liable to Ben and Cat for the value of the painting that he received from Tom *minus* what Ben and Cat are unable to recover from Tom by bringing a claim against him for misapplying assets he was supposed to hold on trust for them. So under the rule Ben and Cat will be required to sue Tom for the value of the painting and see how much they can recover from Tom; if they cannot recover the full value of the painting from Tom (because, for example, he is bankrupt), then Vic will be liable for the rest.

(3) *Liability for unconscionable receipt*. If when receiving the painting from Tom, Vic had sufficient knowledge of the fact that Tom was committing a breach of trust by transferring that painting to Vic, and the painting can no longer be recovered from Vic because Vic does not have it, Vic will be liable to Ben and Cat for the value of the painting 'as a constructive trustee'. How much knowledge is sufficient? Enough that it was 'unconscionable' for Vic to accept the painting from Tom: *BCCI* v *Akindele* [2001] Ch 437, 455 (per Nourse LJ). The same will be true if Vic acquired the painting innocently but before disposing of it, he acquired sufficient knowledge of Tom's breach of trust in giving him the painting that it became unconscionable for Vic to treat the painting as his own to dispose of. If Vic no longer has the painting, he will be liable to Ben and Cat 'as a constructive trustee' for the value of the painting.

(4) *Liability for dishonestly inducing/assisting a breach of trust*. If Dan dishonestly induced, or assisted, Tom to commit a breach of trust by giving the painting to Vic, then Dan will be liable to Ben and Cat 'as a constructive trustee' for the loss suffered by them as a result of Tom's breach of trust: *Eaves* v *Hickson* (1861) 30 Beav 136 (liability for dishonestly procuring a breach of trust); *Royal Brunei Airlines* v *Tan* [1995] 2 AC 378 (liability for dishonestly assisting a breach of trust). Dan will be held to have acted dishonestly in inducing, or assisting, Tom to commit his

breach of trust if an honest person would not have done what Dan did (to induce or assist Tom's breach of trust) had they known what Dan did at the time Dan acted: ibid, 390–91 (per Lord Nicholls).

(5) *Impounding.* If the painting formed part of a larger trust fund that Tom holds on trust for Ben and Cat, and Ben induced Tom to dispose of the painting to Vic in breach of trust, or consented in writing to Tom's doing that, while Cat did not, then only Cat will be able to sue in respect of Tom's breach of trust. And one of the remedies that may be available to Cat is that Cat may be able to have the courts *impound* Ben's interest under the trust fund until the loss caused to the trust fund by Tom's breach of trust is made up: Trustee Act 1925, s 62.

CONSTRUCTIVE TRUSTEE CONFUSIONS

Three confusions have been created by using the phrase 'liable as a constructive trustee' to describe liabilities (3) and (4).

First, the use of the term 'constructive trustee' led people to think that liabilities (3) and (4) had something to do with the law on constructive trusts, so that textbooks and monographs would include (3) and (4) in their categories of situations where a constructive trust would arise (see, for example, Oakley 1997, ch 4). Those days are now gone, helped on their way by Millett LJ's pointing out in *Paragon Finance* v *D B Thakerar & Co* [1999] 1 All ER 400 (at 408) that 'the expressions "constructive trust" and "constructive trustee" … describe two entirely different situations'. A constructive trust is an imposed trust, while (3) and (4) do not describe situations where an imposed trust arises, but rather situations where someone who is not an express trustee will incur a personal liability as a result of a breach of trust having been committed: Smith 1999, 296–301.

Second, the use of the term 'liable as a constructive trustee' to describe *both* liabilities (3) and (4) has created the impression that both liabilities rest on the same basis and the same remedies should be available in respect of each. The Court of Appeal's decision in *Novoship (UK) Ltd* v *Mikhaylyuk* [2015] QB 499 is typical in this regard, casually running together liabilities (3) and (4) when observing (at [68]) that 'Although, for the purpose of legal analysis, it is convenient to distinguish between the two types of secondary liability, a person may be liable under both heads, depending on the facts of a particular case.' Similarly, Millett LJ in the *Paragon Finance* case held that *both* forms of liability arise 'when a defendant is implicated in a fraud. Equity has always given relief against fraud by making any person sufficiently implicated in the fraud accountable in equity' (409).

Third, the use of the term 'liable as a *constructive* trustee' to describe liabilities (3) and (4) has encouraged the view that it is wrong to think of a defendant who incurs either form of liability as being a trustee – that when they are said to be liable as a constructive trustee, the word 'constructive' is being used in the sense of 'fictional' rather than 'imposed'. The defendant is held liable *as though* they were a trustee, not because they *were* a trustee. As Lord Millett observed in *Dubai Aluminium Co Ltd v Salaam* [2003] 2 AC 366 (at [141]), a defendant who incurs liability (3) or (4) 'is not a trustee at all, even though he may be liable to account as if he were. He never claims to assume the position of trustee on behalf of others, and he may be liable without ever receiving or handling the trust property.' This is certainly true of liability (4) – where Dan dishonestly induces, or assists, Tom to commit a breach of trust by giving a painting to Vic, no trust assets come into Dan's hands that Dan could be said to be a trustee of. But it is not at all clear that Vic cannot be said to be a trustee (*de son tort*) of a painting that he has received from Tom with sufficient knowledge that Tom was committing a breach of trust in transferring that painting to her; and it has been argued that this is the basis of liability (3).

Vic incurs liability (3), it has been argued, because Vic held the painting as a trustee when he received it, and is therefore accountable for the value of the painting that he has now wrongfully disposed of: Mitchell and Watterson 2009, Chambers 2016. So Vic is *not* liable in respect of Tom's breach of trust in transferring the painting to Vic, but Vic's *own* breach of trust in failing to preserve the painting in his hands when he held that painting as a trustee. Despite this, the UK Supreme Court held in *Williams* v *Central Bank of Nigeria* [2014] AC 1189, on the basis of observations such as Lord Millett's, that for the purposes of the law on limitation of actions – under which there is no limitation period for suing a trustee who has committed a fraudulent breach of trust or treated trust assets as their own to dispose of (Limitation Act 1980, s 21(1)) – it would be wrong to think that someone who incurred liability (3) was a trustee (see, in particular, [31] (per Lord Sumption) and [64] (per Lord Neuberger)).

FAULT REQUIREMENTS

The law has not done a particularly good job in defining the degree of fault on the part of a defendant that has to be established for them to incur liabilities (3) or (4).

For a while legal academics fell under the spell of Peter Birks' argument that liability (3) should not be based on fault at all, just like liability (2) is not fault-based. He took the view that for a defendant to incur liability (3), it was enough that the defendant received trust assets that had been disposed of in breach of trust. (See, for example, Birks 2002.) In such a case, the defendant would be *unjustly enriched* at the expense of the beneficiaries of the trust 'whose' assets had gone walkabout without their consent. Any harshness involved in holding a defendant recipient of trust assets (disposed of in breach of trust) strictly liable for the value of those assets would be mitigated by allowing the defendant a defence of *change of position* if they dissipated some or all of those assets in good faith.

Birks' argument is now known to be flawed, perhaps fatally so: Smith 2000; Swadling 2019b, 317–22. But it was popular enough at the turn of the century to be adopted by a member of the House of Lords (Nicholls 1998) and for it to be seriously argued in *BCCI v Akindele* [2001] Ch 437 that liability for receipt of trust assets disposed of without authorisation should be strict. That argument was rejected as 'commercially unworkable' (456) as it would expose banks and companies to too many claims, where they had unwittingly taken receipt of trust assets disposed of in breach of trust, that they would find very hard to fend off by reference to a change of position defence. But the standard of liability adopted instead – based on the 'unconscionable' receipt or retention of trust assets disposed of in breach of trust (455) – is hardly satisfactory; in fact, William Swadling called it 'hopeless' (Swadling 2019b, 313). The subsequent observation that a fault requirement of unconscionability is a 'flexible test, which requires the court to consider what is right, taking into account the nature and extent of the defendant's knowledge and all the circumstances relating to the receipt' (*Starglade Properties Ltd v Nash* [2010] EWHC 148 (Ch), [57] (per Strauss QC)) hardly narrows things down as to what 'unconscionable receipt' actually means. The best that can be suggested – in line with the rationale of liability (3) as based on the defendant's breaching a duty that she owed the claimant beneficiaries to protect the trust assets from being dissipated – is that the defendant's state of knowledge must be such as to make it fair to impose on her the burdens of trusteeship.

The fault requirement for liability (4) to be incurred is that the defendant needs to have acted dishonestly in inducing or assisting a trustee to commit a breach of trust, and a defendant will be held to have acted dishonestly if they acted in a way that an honest person would not have done had they known what the defendant knew: *Barlow Clowes Ltd* v *Eurotrust Ltd* [2006] 1 WLR 1476, [15]–[16] (per Lord Hoffmann); *Group Seven Ltd* v *Nasir* [2020] Ch 129, [58]. The problem with this test is that it is circular: what is dishonest is defined in terms of what an honest person would do (if they knew what the defendant knew). Lord Nicholls might have been able in the *Tan* case to say 'Honest people do not intentionally deceive others to their detriment. Honest people do not knowingly take others' property. Unless there is a very good and compelling reason, an honest person does not participate in a transaction if he knows it involves a misapplication of trust assets to the detriment of the beneficiaries. Nor does an honest person in such a case deliberately close his eyes and ears, or deliberately not ask questions, lest he learn something he would rather not know, and then proceed regardless' ([1995] 2 AC 378, 389). But in cases where we are seriously in doubt as to whether a defendant has acted dishonestly, a test for dishonesty that invites us to reflect on what an honest person would have done is useless: we would not be uncertain as to whether the defendant acted dishonestly if we knew what an honest person would have done.

Faced with this difficulty, it is unsurprising that Paul Davies has recently argued that making a defendant's liability under (4) turn on their honesty (or lack thereof) is a mistake, and that the law should revert to where it stood before *Tan*, when liability (4) turned on the state of the defendant's *knowledge* (however defined): Davies 2022, 47–57. One problem with restricting liability (4) to cases where the defendant knowingly induced/assisted a breach of trust (other than being unable to define satisfactorily what degree of knowledge is required: see *Tan* [1995] 2 AC 378, 391) is that liability (4) would seemingly no longer cover someone who had no reason to think that they were assisting/inducing *a breach of trust* but were still acting dishonestly because they thought they were assisting/inducing some kind of nefarious scheme. Millett argued strongly that liability (4) should cover this kind of case in *Agip (Africa) Ltd* v *Jackson* [1990] 1 Ch 265, 295: 'It is no defence for a man charged with having … assisted in a fraudulent and dishonest scheme to say that he thought it was "only" a breach of exchange controls or "only" a case of tax evasion.' Charles Mitchell is of the same view: 'it is hard to agree that a defendant who knows or has good grounds for suspecting that he has assisted in fraudulent behaviour of some kind should be absolved from liability towards the claimant he has actually helped to defraud, because he did not know who his victim was, or because he thought he was defrauding someone else' (Mitchell 2002, 198).

Perhaps the dishonesty standard for incurring liability (4) can be saved by the recent suggestion that what counts as dishonest turns on the standards of 'ordinary decent people' (*Ivey* v *Genting Casinos (UK) Ltd* [2018] AC 391, [74] (per Lord Hughes)). This raises the prospect that a judge (who can be presumed to be an ordinary decent person, and whose friends and neighbours can be presumed to be ordinary decent people) could determine whether a given defendant has acted dishonestly by asking 'If I had done what the defendant did, knowing what the defendant knew, would I rather that my friends and neighbours didn't know what I had done?' If the answer is 'I'd rather they didn't know' then the defendant can be said to have acted dishonestly by the standards of ordinary decent people.

5

Pandora's Box

In a previous *Key Ideas* book, on the law of contract, I discussed how the law of contract enables markets to exist (McBride 2017, ch 2). Given this, no one could seriously question whether we should have a law of contract or its value, despite the excesses and abuses that the existence of contract law can give rise to. Lord Mansfield thought the same could be said of trusts law, remarking in *Burgess v Wheate* (1759) 1 Black W 123, at 160 that 'Trusts are made to answer the exigencies of families and all purposes, without producing one inconvenience, fraud, or private mischief which the Statute [of Uses] meant to avoid.' This seems overly optimistic.

The value of the law of trusts is much more questionable than that of the law of contract, and it is possible to argue that Henry VIII might have been onto something when he attempted to kill off trusts in their earlier incarnation through the Statute of Uses. As Lord Millett has observed extra-judicially (Willoughby 2002, i): 'By the last decades of the [20th] century [the trust] had, like Odysseus and Aeneas, descended into the underworld … [It] was employed by international fraudsters, drug traffickers and tax evaders to launder their ill-gotten gains and conceal the source and ownership of their money. Such settlors demanded anonymity, mobility and flexibility. Hence arose the trust which a client of [mine] once described … as "a non-domiciliary, non-beneficial, discretionary migratory trust." (He was arrested soon afterwards.)'

It is, of course, now impossible to extirpate the concept of a trust from common law legal systems – but appreciating the extent of the harms caused by the existence of trusts law is an essential precursor to taking steps to mitigate those harms. What those harms are, and what steps might be taken to curtail them, is the subject matter of this concluding chapter.

1. FRAUD

It is said that 'A fool and their money are soon parted' and a trust is one of the devices by which the parting is effected, by giving a conman's mark the false assurance that they can safely entrust their assets to the conman. This is what happened in *Hodgson* v *Marks* [1971] 1 Ch 892.

Hodgson was a widow who had been living in the same house for about 20 years. She took in a lodger, Evans, who soon became trusted enough by Hodgson that she would give him small amounts of money to invest for her. Evans started pestering Hodgson about his worries that her nephew would try to turn him out of the house. Eventually, Hodgson gave in to Evans' suggestion that she convey her house to him, to be held on trust for her, as a way of securing his position in the house. Of course, as soon as Evans obtained title to the house, he sold it to Marks – to whom it came as an unpleasant surprise after he had paid £6,000 for the house (almost £100,000 in today's money) to find Hodgson living in it and claiming that the house was held on trust for her.

Hodgson was lucky – the presumption that land which is transferred to a stranger as a gift is intended to be held on trust for the donor (p 11) came to her aid, allowing her to establish that title to the house was held on trust for her by Evans, despite the lack of any writing to prove that; the court went on to hold that Marks bought the house subject to Hodgson's rights by virtue of her being in actual occupation of the house when he bought it. So it ended up being Marks, rather than Hodgson, who proved to be the victim of Evans' con – but it was a confidence trick that Evans simply could not have pulled off if the institution of the trust did not exist.

Others are induced to part with their money by the promise that if they invest their money in a particular fund or scheme, those running the fund or scheme will hold the money as trustees, and consequently have a duty to invest the money with a professional degree of care and skill so as to make more money for the investor. Three such cases can be distinguished.

In the first, the trustees are dishonest. They are running a Ponzi scheme where they appropriate investors' monies for themselves and keep up the appearance of properly investing their investors' monies through fake accounts and payouts derived from new investors putting capital into the fund. When the scheme collapses, as it invariably does, investors will find that most, if not all, of their money has disappeared. This first type of case is rare, which is why people who run such schemes, such as Bernard Madoff (whose Ponzi scheme ran for over 30 years, collapsing in the aftermath of the 2008 economic crisis, with losses to investors of $18 billion (reduced to $4 billion after legal actions)), acquire such notoriety.

The second kind of case is far more common. In this kind of case, the trustees promise investors that through the application of a new-fangled algorithm or their skill in analysing market trends, they will achieve high returns for their investors. These hopes are almost invariably disappointed. Hardly anyone can be a Michael Burry, of *The Big Short* (Lewis 2011) fame, who was able to spot (along with some others) that the US housing market was on the verge of a precipitous decline and by 'shorting' the housing market made returns of almost 500 per cent for those investing in his Scion Capital hedge fund. Instead, it is far more likely that the trustees will be unable to 'outperform the market' – that is, achieve higher returns than would be the case if the investors' money simply tracked the movement of the stock market as a whole: Molloy 2009, 544–47; Malkiel 2020, ch 7. (On the general incompetence of managers to achieve the results that they are supposed to be experts in achieving, see McBride 2020, 102.)

In the worst cases – such as the collapse in 1998 of the Long Term Capital Management hedge fund (see Lowenstein 2001) – investors lose all or most of their money. In the best cases, investors make very poor returns on their money – in one study over the 10-year period from 2005 to 2015, a 2 per cent annual return compared with the 6 per cent annual return that money invested in an index tracking the stock market would have earned (Shaxson 2019, 210). (Over 10 years, the difference between the two returns results in an initial investment of £100 turning into £122 at 2 per cent, and £182 at 6 per cent – a 50 per cent difference.) But in the meantime, the trustees do very well, charging *annual* fees equivalent to 6–13 per cent of the value of the fund they are administering (ibid, 212). Although the trustees may be honest, their investors are still entitled to feel defrauded. As the Wall Street joke has it, people are persuaded to hand over their money through the promise of high returns but 'Where are the customers' yachts?' (ibid, 213) – only the trustees end up making enough money to be able to buy a yacht.

The third case is by now the most common. Recognising their general incapacity to outperform the market, the trustees do not attempt for the most part to invest the trust fund 'actively' – buying shares that they think are undervalued and selling shares that they think are overvalued. Instead, the trustees invest the trust fund 'passively', ploughing the trust funds into index or tracker funds that are designed to match the overall movements of stock markets. Writing in 1996, John Langbein estimated that 'hundreds of billions' of American dollars were invested in tracker funds (Langbein 1996, 658). The reality nowadays far exceeds that figure. The biggest providers of tracker funds in the United States nowadays are Blackrock, which manages $10 trillion worth of assets, Vanguard ($7 trillion) and State Street Corporation ($3 trillion). Marxist thinkers and politicians used to talk about having governments seize the 'commanding heights' of the economy, so as to make companies and markets work for the public good. In only a few years, companies such as Blackrock and Vanguard have managed to gain control of those commanding heights, simply because trustees across the world know of no other better or more reliable way of achieving decent returns for their investors than to invest in index or tracker funds – and Blackrock and Vanguard have been able to cater for that demand by using the money funnelled to them by trustees to acquire significant shareholdings in every major public company in the world, which shareholdings then form the basis of the index or tracker funds that the trustees are invested in via extended chains of intermediated securities (p 17).

The result has been described as 'worse than Marxism' (Lowrey 2021). One of the most significant economic harms caused by so many shares being the subject of passive investing is linked with the role that the price of a share is supposed to play in how a company is run. The price of a share in a company is supposed to reflect the company's projected earnings – the higher the projected future earnings, the higher the price; the lower, the lower the price. So if a company's projected future earnings decline, so should its share price, thus triggering two effects: (i) the current shareholders in the company will see their wealth decrease and will be accordingly incentivised to discipline the directors of the company, so as to try to increase the company's projected earnings; (ii) outside investors will see that the company is cheaper to acquire, and will be accordingly incentivised to bid for it, again with a view to turning the company's fortunes around. So downward movements in a company's share price are a stimulus to the company's being run more efficiently. However, when a large number of a company's shares are held passively – simply because that company happens to be in the top 100 companies listed on the London or New York Stock Exchange – it becomes harder for that company's shares to lose value, as there are fewer such shares available for active trading. As a result, no one has any incentive to take any action to ensure that the company is run efficiently so as to maximise its projected earnings.

Another significant economic harm caused by widespread passive investing is a decrease in competition between different companies operating in the same market, resulting in the prices for those companies' goods and services drifting upwards (and the quality of those goods and services drifting downwards) in a way that would not be possible were those companies seriously competing with each other. If a significant number of shares in *each* of those companies is owned by a company like Blackrock, Blackrock will have no reason to encourage any of those companies to do anything that might undercut a rival's earnings – as whatever Blackrock wins in terms of the undercutting company's share price going up will be offset by the decline in the undercut company's share price. And even if this were not the case, Blackrock would still have no reason to encourage competition between the companies in which it is invested, as it is simply not interested in increasing the value of its shares – its only interest is in being invested in a representative set of companies and letting the market do its thing in terms of growing the value of that investment over time.

But it is doubtful whether the market can do anything to grow the value of an investment in the absence of the incentives and disciplines that applied to inflate and deflate the value of companies' shareholdings in the age before passive investing became widespread. It may be, then, that passive investing is a real-life example of the story of the goose that laid golden eggs. In order to get at all of the golden eggs that he was sure were inside the goose, the farmer who owned the goose killed it – and there were no more golden eggs for him. In the same way, it became clear in the 1970s that passive investing in the stock market would produce higher returns than active investing (or 'stock picking'). But those higher returns will disappear the more funds are invested passively, as passive investing will tend to have the effect of freezing companies' share prices, and the wider economy will begin to rot and decay.

It seems, then, that the only way for trust beneficiaries not to be defrauded by those who are supposed to invest trust assets for them is for the trustees to adopt an investment strategy that, if widely replicated, will not only prove extremely harmful economically, but which also tends to resemble a pyramid scheme, where only the early entrants to the scheme profit, at the expense of later entrants. Fraud, in one form or another, therefore seems inextricably associated with trusts, at least where those trusts involve a trustee's investing money for another with a view to making money for them.

2. WEALTH MANAGEMENT

What have become known as 'wealth managers' need not worry about *making* money for their clients. As Brooke Harrington observes in her pioneering study of how wealth managers operate, 'Ordinarily, wealth managers are employed by clients who have already accumulated their fortunes, so the professional's job is less to increase the value of those assets than to protect them from dissipation at the hands of tax authorities, creditors, and heirs. This defensive orientation gives the profession an unusual position within the finance industry, which is otherwise associated with aggressive profit seeking' (Harrington 2020, 10; also 137).

The trust is the wealth manager's weapon of choice in trying to achieve the goals of helping their clients avoid paying tax and protecting the client's assets from their creditors – and offshore is where the battle to achieve those goals is waged.

We have already noted (p 21) how, beginning with the Cook Islands in the South Pacific, a number of jurisdictions now allow settlors to prevent creditors accessing their assets by salting them away in an 'asset protection' trust. As a result, 'Fannie Mae, a government sponsored lender ... only recovered $12,000 of a $10 million judgment against an Oklahoma developer who defaulted on his loans because his assets were tied up in a Cook Islands trust, and the Federal Trade Commission ... has been unable to recover its $37.5 million judgment against Kevin Trudeau for deceiving consumers with a book called *The Weight Loss Cure* because Trudeau's assets are in a Cook Islands trust' (Barnett 2022, 375–76). Harrington explains that 'To date, no effort to break a Cook Islands asset protection trust has been successful. Many creditors don't even try, since pursuing a claim against a trust based there requires litigating in the Cook Islands; this means sending a legal team on a long and costly journey – fifteen hours of flight time from New York, plus billable hours' (Harrington

2020, 158; though on the question of whether a Cook Islands asset protection trust has ever been 'broken' see Smith 2018, 2160–61).

Attempts to break asset protection trusts in other jurisdictions have been more successful. In *Tasarruf Mevduati Sigorta Fonu* v *Merrill Lynch Bank and Trust Co Ltd* [2012] 1 WLR 1721, the claimant obtained judgment against the defendant for $30 million in Turkey, where the defendant had no assets and was declared bankrupt. The claimant sought to enforce the judgment debt that the defendant owed him by accessing a $24 million Cayman Islands discretionary trust that had been created by the defendant, with the beneficiaries of the trust being the defendant and his wife; the trust could also be revoked by the defendant. The defendant argued that as the $24 million was held on a discretionary trust, he did not technically have any rights over the $24 million, only a right to be considered as a future donee of some or all of that money (p 33), and so the $24 million could not be accessed to pay off the debt he owed the claimant. The Privy Council disagreed, holding that the defendant's power to revoke the discretionary trust meant that he could 'be regarded as having rights tantamount to ownership' ([59]) of the $24 million, with the result that an order could be made against him requiring him to exercise that power and make the $24 million available to satisfy the claimant's claim.

The discretionary trust is one of the principal devices by which wealth managers help their clients avoid paying taxes on their assets. (Discretionary trusts have been associated for so long with tax avoidance that Harman LJ was able to say almost 60 years ago, in argument in *Re Londonderry's Settlement* [1965] Ch 918 (at 927), 'I think a discretionary trust is merely a fiscal dodge.') By settling assets on a discretionary trust, the settlor can claim to have that they no longer have any rights over those assets with the result that they are no longer liable to pay tax on them. But the settlor still effectively controls those assets, via either a letter of wishes supplied to the trustee, or (in offshore jurisdictions) by empowering a 'protector' of the trust to direct the trustee how to exercise their powers under the discretionary trust and reserving to the settlor the power to direct the protector how to do this. The discretionary trusts that formed the basis of the litigation in *Schmidt* v *Rosewood Trust Ltd* [2003] 2 AC 709 are typical examples of a discretionary trust created for the purpose of tax avoidance.

The discretionary trusts in that case were created in the Isle of Man by Vitali Schmidt, 'a senior executive of Lukoil, which is the largest oil company in Russia and one of the largest oil companies in the world' ([4]). About $105 million was settled on these discretionary trusts. Any monies not distributed to the potential beneficiaries under the discretionary trust would go to a charity, the Royal National Lifeboat Institution. But it was never intended that the RNLI would obtain anything under the trust, and indeed the RNLI would never have heard of the trust (Shaxson 2019, 173–74; Smith 2017). As best as anyone can tell, the reasons for making a charity the default beneficiary under these kinds of discretionary trusts (sometimes known as 'Red Cross trusts' because the Red Cross charity is often the default beneficiary under them) are (i) to ensure that no one can argue that the settlor was intended to be the default beneficiary (thus potentially making them liable for tax on the trust assets); (ii) to ensure that it could not be argued that the trust offended against the 'beneficiary principle' (p 27); (iii) to take advantage of any tax breaks and laxer rules against money laundering that come into play when a charity is involved. Instead, the real beneficiaries who were supposed to benefit under the discretionary trust were listed in a schedule that only the trustees had access to, and the trustees had the power to make anyone else a potential beneficiary of the trust. However, the trustees' powers to distribute property under the trust to beneficiaries could only be exercised with the consent of the 'protector' of the trust – where the protector was named as Vitali Schmidt, the settlor. The protector was also able to keep the trustees of the trust in line by virtue of having the power to appoint and dismiss them.

The same trick – of effectively controlling how trust assets are deployed while ensuring that the settlor and anyone who might benefit under the trust can claim not to have any rights over those assets, which might then make them liable for tax on those assets – can be pulled through the creation of a non-charitable purpose trust. We have seen that, with some exceptions, this is not possible under English law (p 43), but as the example of STAR trusts shows (p 21), offshore trust jurisdictions have been bolder in this regard, in order to attract wealth from abroad.

The harm done by asset protection trusts is to justice – as Lionel Smith observes, recognising that asset protection trusts are valid involves the law in a 'self-destruction of legal values. One and the same legal system says that a person owes money but does not have to pay' (Smith 2018, 2172). The harm done by tax avoidance through trusts is far more serious. Forcing governments to operate on smaller budgets and higher deficits than would be the case if the option of transferring one's money offshore were not on the table does not just harm the justice system (for example, by making it impossible to provide proper levels of legal aid for those who cannot afford legal services themselves) but every form of public service, and loads future generations with government debts that they will find it impossible to repay. Writing in 2015, Gabriel Zucman estimated that the world's financial wealth came to $95.5 trillion, and out of that sum $7.6 trillion (8 per cent) was held offshore in tax havens (Zucman 2015, 35). He went on to estimate that 'the artificial shifting of profits to low-tax locales enables US companies to reduce their tax liabilities, in total, by about $130 billion a year' (ibid, 105). Richard Murphy estimates that the same form of tax avoidance costs the UK government £5 billion a year (Murphy 2017, 115). (By comparison, the total budget for legal aid in England and Wales in 2020–21 was £1.5 billion.) As we will see in the next section, these sums are dwarfed by the sums lost not to tax avoidance but to tax *evasion*, using trusts and other devices in offshore tax havens to keep secret from the taxman one's rights over assets.

Harrington's study shows that a lot of wealth managers are unapologetic about their role in enabling their clients to avoid taxes, as they regard the paying of taxes to governments as throwing good money after bad (Harrington 2020, 136; also Shaxson 2012, 230): far better to keep wealth in private hands, where it can be used productively and not wasted. Others feel less comfortable with this role, and while they are strongly encouraged to keep their thoughts to themselves (Shaxson 2012, 219–37) they can console themselves with the third aspect of a wealth manager's role – after helping their clients avoid taxes and creditors – which is helping the client do their best for their family. As one disaffected wealth manager explained 'there were always cases where you could believe you were helping someone. For example, countries like Brazil have forced heirship, which dictates who in a family gets the assets after parents die, and an offshore trust may be a way to get around this … [In one case] forced heirship would have granted the assets to a playboy son, instead of to the family's preferred beneficiary, a daughter with special needs' (ibid, 218). This kind of work takes trusts law back to its origins, to the desire to circumvent rules preventing someone determining who would inherit their property after they died (p 8). As Maitland observed, trusts got their start (as uses) because of an Englishman's desire 'to provide for his daughters and younger sons' (Maitland 1905, 84).

3. FOSTERING CRIMINALITY

Much of what we know about the world of offshore trusts is down to three leaks of confidential financial information: the leak of the 'Panama Papers' in 2015, the 'Paradise Papers' in 2017, and the 'Pandora Papers' in 2021. The Panama Papers consist in 11.5 million documents leaked from the Panamanian law firm Mossack Fonseca. The Paradise Papers are made up of 13.4 million documents, principally derived from the global law firm Appleby, which specialises in providing offshore services to clients. The Pandora Papers are much more wide-ranging, consisting in 11.9 million documents derived from 14 different financial services providers. (The International Consortium of Investigative Journalists ('ICIJ') – which helped break the story of the leaks of all these papers – maintains a website at offshoreleaks.icij.org that allows people to search for information in, and about, these papers.)

While much of the information provided by these leaks reveals lawful, though embarrassing, attempts by politicians, companies and holier than thou celebrities to avoid tax through the use of offshore devices, when the original 'John Doe' (whose identity has never been discovered, even by the journalists that they contacted) who leaked the Panama Papers was asked 'Why are you taking this risk?' they responded, 'I feel I must do it because I'm able. It's too important. There is just a mind-boggling amount of criminal activity going on here – I struggle to even wrap my head around it' (Obermayer and Obermaier 2017, 22). That criminal activity represents the trust's descent into the underworld referred to by Lord Millett in the quotation at the start of this chapter.

What makes the trust an ideal vehicle for (a) committing crimes, such as bribery or tax evasion, and (b) handling the proceeds of crime, in particular through money laundering, is that 'Trusts can shroud assets in cast-iron secrecy' (Shaxson 2012, 42). Nicholas Shaxson points out that 'If you have a million dollars in a trust in Jersey and the tax inspectors come after you, it will be hard for them even to start their enquiries as trust instruments in Jersey are not registered in any official or public register' (ibid). And the secrecy surrounding the trust can be made 'deeper still, by layering one secrecy structure on top of another. The asset held in the Jersey trust may be a million dollars sitting in a bank in Panama, itself protected by strong bank secrecy … [T]he tax inspectors … could never get the Jersey lawyer to reveal the beneficiary because they wouldn't necessarily know it; they merely send the cheques to another lawyer somewhere else, who also isn't the beneficiary. And you can keep on going: you can layer a trust in Jersey on another trust in the Cayman Islands, then perch that on top of a secretive company structure in Delaware' (Shaxson 2012, 43). Given the secrecy that surrounds trusts, it is not surprising that 'When the World Bank carried out a survey of how criminals use legal structures to hide stolen assets, it said trusts were so difficult to investigate or prosecute that they were rarely prioritised in corruption investigations, because they were so hard to crack open' (Shaxson 2019, 175, citing World Bank 2011, 44–47).

In their account of how they were leaked the Panama Papers, the journalists Bastian Obermayer and Frederik Obermaier provide a couple of examples from the Panama Papers of trusts being used for criminal purposes. First, money laundering. 'A client gets in touch [with Mossack Fonseca] because he wants to cash a couple of cheques worth $100,000, but without leaving "a trail" to him or his company ... One of the suggestions made is to put the money in an anonymous trust, which then buys shares in a company, which makes a donation to the client' (Obermayer and Obermaier 2017, 145). Second, tax evasion. '[A] client has accumulated quite a fortune through business deals in the USA and Sweden. A little over €2 million and 1 million Swiss francs are sitting in a number of Swiss accounts ... [The client] wants to transfer this money to an investment account in Panama ... The money appears to be transferred in several instalments from one account – which is ... not in [the client's name] but in that of a shell company – to a trust company which in turn transfers it to Andbank Panama ... another trust company. The instructions state that ... it is vital that the name of the account holder does not appear on the transfer' (Obermayer and Obermaier 2017, 147). Gabriel Zucman estimated in 2015 that the hiding of wealth in offshore jurisdictions to evade taxation results in a $190 billion yearly shortfall in tax receipts across the world (Zucman 2015, 48), with the United States losing out on $35 billion a year, and Europe $78 billion a year (ibid, 53). Richard Murphy estimated in 2011 that the global shortfall in tax receipts due to tax evasion was far higher: $3.1 *trillion* a year (Murphy 2017, 109).

4. THE CURSE OF TRUSTS?

Nicholas Shaxson raises an important question, which is whether the ability to create trusts under English law results in jurisdictions based on English law being subjected to a 'resource curse': Shaxson 2019, 4–9. The idea of a 'resource curse' goes as follows: a country in which a rare and valuable resource is located can actually be made worse off because of that fact. In a previous book, I explained the mechanism by which a resource curse operates (McBride 2020, 18). If *Silvania* is 'blessed' with abundant supplies of a particularly valuable element (call it 'silvanium') that is difficult to find elsewhere in the world, other countries will have every incentive to try to guarantee a reliable supply of silvanium by bribing a political group within *Silvania* to seize power, and use *Silvania's* supplies of silvanium for the benefit of that group and those other countries – and not for the benefit of *Silvania's* general population. So simply by virtue of being abundantly supplied with a resource that everyone else wants, *Silvania* ends up being ruled by a corrupt dictatorship that is focussed on enriching itself and other countries, while entrenching itself in power by repressing *Silvania's* general population.

Shaxson's suggestion is that a legal system that empowers the creation of trusts may be subject to a resource curse. The fact that wealth can be held on trust under that legal system is valuable to wealthy people living in other countries (*offshore*), with the result that those people use their wealth to try to capture that legal system, and ensure that its trusts law starts working for *them*, rather than the general (*onshore*) population that is governed by that legal system. This is not a bad description of what seems to have happened in trust law jurisdictions. As Brooke Harrington observes 'the evidence from tax havens suggests that states can be hacked so that they become instruments of foreign elites' (Harrington 2020, 262). Bearing this point out, she reports on an encounter with a local fisherman in the Cook Islands. Talking about the wealth management industry, he said 'They're why everyone calls us the "Crook Islands" now: they've got our government in their pockets. I hate what they've done to my country' (ibid, 247).

Moving geographically closer to the country from where trusts law originated, the island of Jersey estimates that it holds £1 *trillion* worth of assets on trust, principally on discretionary trusts (Shaxson 2019, 174). The finance industry has taken over Jersey, accounting for over 90 per cent of government revenue and employing 25 per cent of the Jersey workforce (Shaxson 2012, 237; see also Harrington 2020, 246–47). It has become so important that those who are unhappy with finance industry practices can be cowed into silence through threats of being sacked and made unemployable (Shaxson 2012, 235). As one Jersey inhabitant observed, 'We live in a dictatorship. This is not a democratic country' (ibid). Nicholas Shaxson comments, 'To the casual visitor, Jersey looks and feels very British. But it is very, very different from the Britain I know' (ibid). But the curse of trusts may be making Britain much more like Jersey. Nicholas Shaxson reports that 'little more than 10 per cent of UK bank lending goes to businesses outside the financial sector' with the result that 'Investment in the non-financial parts of the UK economy has been less than that of Italy' (Shaxson 2019, 8) and 'on an income-per-person basis, Britain's economy is smaller than that of nearly all of its northern European peers, and its productivity is a full 25 per cent lower than … France' (ibid, 9). He estimates that if the UK did not have such an 'oversized financial sector' the country as a whole would be £4.5 trillion *better off* than it is today (ibid, 11).

If there is such a thing as a 'trusts curse', attempts to mitigate it have principally focussed on trying to address problems of tax evasion by making people's holdings of wealth on trust more transparent. This is done either through requiring financial institutions to report on whether they are holding wealth for nationals of a particular country (as, in the United States, under the Foreign Account Tax Compliance Act (FATCA)) or by requiring trusts to be registered (as under reg 45 of the Money Laundering, Terrorist Financing and Transfer of Funds (Information on the Payer) Regulations 2017; on which, see Brown 2022). However, as we have seen, the harms caused by trusts law range much more widely than just enabling tax evasion, and we can be skeptical about the political will to tackle those harms when the political class is itself so dependent for its funding on support from the financial sector. If the 'trusts curse' is to be arrested or even reversed, the initiative must come from the people who were responsible for trusts law existing in the first place – the judges. There are a variety of initiatives that the judges might take that might have some impact on the damaging trends that have started to operate within trusts law over the last 50 years.

First, the courts could place a renewed emphasis on the 'irreducible core of a trust'. For example, they could refuse to recognise as trusts: (i) trusts where the beneficiaries have no realistic prospect of being able to invoke their rights under the rule in *Saunders* v *Vautier* to demand that the trust assets be transferred to them; or (ii) trusts where the beneficiaries are unaware that they are beneficiaries. Such a reform would have the effect of invalidating the 'Red Cross' discretionary trusts (or, in Lionel Smith's terms, 'massively discretionary trusts': Smith 2017) that seem to comprise a large proportion of Jersey's trust holdings, and which seem to exist purely for the basis of tax avoidance. The courts could also rule that (iii) a trust that can be revoked by the settlor at will is no trust at all. Again, this would have the effect of invalidating trusts that are designed to hide assets behind a trust from the settlor's creditors, and allow them to be reclaimed by the settlor when the coast is clear.

Second, the courts could inject new life into the maxim that 'he who comes to equity must do so with clean hands' – the idea being that you cannot ask Equity's assistance in enforcing some right or other if you yourself are guilty of some form of inequitable conduct (see, generally, McBride 2018). The prospect that their attempts to enforce a trust might be denied on the grounds of 'unclean hands' would provide a major deterrent to settlors' attempting to create a trust for the purpose of tax avoidance or protection from their creditors. That someone acting for the purpose of tax avoidance might be regarded as having unclean hands was suggested by Lord Walker in *Pitt* v *Holt* [2013] 2 AC 108.

That case concerned when a trustee of a discretionary trust would be able to reclaim assets that it had distributed on the ground that it had made a mistake in doing so, where the mistake in the cases considered in *Pitt* v *Holt* was a failure to appreciate properly the tax implications of the distribution that had been made. Lord Walker suggested (at [135]) that it was a live issue whether the courts' power to reverse a distribution of assets under a discretionary trust should be exercised to rescue 'claimants from a tax-avoidance scheme which had gone wrong.' Such a scheme would 'hardly [be] an exercise in good citizenship' and 'In some cases of artificial tax avoidance the courts might think it right to refuse relief … on the grounds of public policy [given that] … artificial tax avoidance is a social evil which puts an unfair burden on the shoulders of those who do not adopt such measures.'

Third, it used to be the case that a trustee could only be sued for a failure to make money for the beneficiaries of the trust if the trustee was in 'wilful default' of their duties under the trust, with 'wilful default' being interpreted as involving either 'wilful neglect in the managing' of the trust assets or (more restrictively) 'very supine negligence' in performing their duties under the trust: Getzler 2002, 44–45. It might be thought that returning to those days would be a disastrous tactic, on the ground that it would embolden trustees to take excessive risks when investing trust assets. But the existing law hardly restrains trustees from taking such risks (see, further, Getzler 2009b), and – as we have already seen – where they do restrain themselves from taking such risks, they do so in ways that are extremely harmful to the wider economy. A return to the old standard for trustees' liability for failing to make a gain for their beneficiaries would be a salutary reminder to settlors and beneficiaries alike that if they want to make more money through investing their existing wealth, they might be better off doing that themselves, following 'the simple ground rule: "we won't invest in anything we don't understand"' (Molloy 2009, 565).

ACKNOWLEDGEMENTS

I should begin by acknowledging the intellectual debt I owe to a murderers' row of academic trusts lawyers who started assembling each week on Zoom for a couple of hours during the COVID-19 lockdowns to keep each other company and chat about topics of mutual interest: Rob Chambers, Josh Getzler, James Penner, Lionel Smith, Rob Stevens and Bill Swadling. Together with Fred Wilmot-Smith and the late, lamented Steve Smith, I was privileged to be invited to join in their sessions and listen to their fascinating debates about various aspects of trusts law. I have tried to ensure this book is one that they would think is worthy of their subject. As the Bibliography shows, it certainly could not have been written without the signal, and very different, contributions they have each made to our knowledge of trusts law.

Another debt is to someone I have never met – Jeffrey Hackney, and his amazing book *Understanding Equity and Trusts*, which was published in 1987, the year before I went to Oxford as an undergraduate to study Law. I remember reading the book as an undergraduate and marvelling at how such a short book could tell me so much more, and of so much more value, than other, much longer, books that I had read. Hackney's book is very much one of the inspirations behind the *Key Ideas* series of books – and if I have come anywhere close to writing something half as good as his book, I will be very pleased.

Hackney once wrote a brilliant book review that concluded with the plea 'no more *Snells*' (Hackney 2001, 154). No one would ever say 'No more Hackneys' – as many Hackneys as possible are very much needed nowadays. Of the 146 works listed in this book's Bibliography, only 14 were available in 1987; of the 144 cases mentioned in this book, exactly a third (48) were decided after 1987. This reflects the explosion of writing, interest and controversy around trusts law in the last 35 years or so. This explosion makes it imperative that students have available to them guides like this one to help them master a subject that has grown hugely since I had to study it, while the time available to students to master the subject remains exactly the same as I had all those years ago.

Kate Whetter at Hart Publishing has proved a huge source of support and encouragement both in expanding the *Key Ideas* project to cover more and more titles, and in the writing of this particular book. Paul Davies and Rory Gregson kindly read and commented on some of the chapters in this book. I am particularly grateful to my personal trainer, Eddie Halls, and my reflexologist, Yumi Matsumoto, for keeping me fit, well and pain-free both generally, and in the course of the very unhealthy process of writing this book for hours on end at my desk.

BIBLIOGRAPHY

Agnew, S and Douglas, S (2019) 'Self-declarations of Trust' 135 *Law Quarterly Review* 67.

Alexander, GS (2013) 'The Dilution of the Trust' in Smith (ed), *The Worlds of the Trust* (Cambridge University Press).

Amnesty International (2016) *This Is What We Die For: Human Rights Abuses in the Democratic Republic of Congo Power the Global Trade in Cobalt* (Amnesty International Ltd).

Baker, JH (2019) *An Introduction to English Legal History*, 5th edn (Oxford University Press).

Barnett, K (2022) 'Offshore Trusts in the South Pacific' in Liew and Harding (eds), *Asia-Pacific Trusts Law Volume 1: Theory and Practice in Context* (Hart Publishing).

Baxendale-Walker, P (1999) *Purpose Trusts* (Butterworths).

Beever, A (2017) 'Engagement, Criticism and the Academic Lawyer' 27 *New Zealand Universities Law Review* 79.

Birks, PBH (1989) *An Introduction to the Law of Restitution*, rev'd edn (Oxford University Press).

—— (1992) 'Restitution and Resulting Trusts' in Goldstein (ed), *Equity and Contemporary Legal Developments* (Hebrew University of Jerusalem).

—— (1994) 'Proprietary Rights as Remedies' in Birks (ed), *The Frontiers of Liability, Volume 2* (Oxford University Press).

—— (1996) 'Equity in the Modern Law: An Exercise in Taxonomy' 26 *University of Western Australia Law Review* 1.

—— (1998) 'The End of the Remedial Constructive Trust?' 12 *Trust Law International* 202.

—— (2002) 'Receipt' in Birks and Pretto (eds), *Breach of Trust* (Hart Publishing).

Brown, L (2022) 'Registering Express Trusts: A Necessary Clarification or Step Too Far?' 28 *Trusts & Trustees* 664.

Chambers, R (1997) *Resulting Trusts* (Oxford University Press).

—— (2002) 'Liability' in Birks and Pretto (eds), *Breach of Trust* (Hart Publishing).

—— (2016) 'The End of Knowing Receipt' 2 *Canadian Journal of Comparative and Contemporary Law* 1.

Chan, K (2016) *The Public-Private Nature of Charity Law* (Hart Publishing).

Clarry, D (2018) *The Supervisory Jurisdiction Over Trust Administration* (Oxford University Press).

Conaglen, M (2010) *Fiduciary Loyalty: Protecting the Due Performance of Non-Fiduciary Duties* (Hart Publishing).

Cretney, S (1969) 'The Rationale of *Keech* v *Sandford*' 33 *Conveyancer & Property Lawyer (New Series)* 161.

Davies, PS (2015) *Accessory Liability* (Hart Publishing).

—— (2018) 'Compensatory Remedies for Breach of Trust' in Nolan, Low and Wu (eds), *Trusts and Modern Wealth Management* (Cambridge University Press).

—— (2022) 'The Mental Element of Accessory Liability in Equity' 138 *Law Quarterly Review* 32.

Donald, MS (2020) 'The Pension Fund as a "Virtual" Institution' in Agnew, Davies and Mitchell (eds), *Pensions: Law, Policy and Practice* (Hart Publishing).

Douglas, A (2021) 'Trusts, Formalities and the Doctrine in *Rochefoucauld* v *Boustead*' *Conveyancer & Property Lawyer* 128.

Edelman, J (2013) 'Two Fundamental Questions for the Law of Trusts' 129 *Law Quarterly Review* 66.

Edelman, J and Elliott, S (2004) 'Money Remedies Against Trustees' 18 *Trusts Law International* 116.

Elliott, S (2002) 'Remoteness Criteria in Equity' 65 *Modern Law Review* 588.

—— (2020) 'Personal Monetary Claims' in McGhee and Elliott (eds), *Snell's Equity*, 34th edn (Sweet & Maxwell).

Fee, J (2020) 'Trust-Owned Companies and the Irreducible Core of the Trust' 26 *Trusts & Trustees* 826.

Finn, PD (1977) *Fiduciary Obligations* (Law Book Company).

Fuller (1941) 'Consideration and Form' 41 *Columbia Law Review* 799.

Gardner, J (2000) 'The Virtue of Charity and its Foils' in Mitchell and Moody (eds), *Foundations of Charity* (Hart Publishing).

Georgiou, AYS (2021) 'Taking Trusts Seriously' 137 *Law Quarterly Review* 305.

Getzler, J (2002) 'Duty of Care' in Birks and Pretto (eds), *Breach of Trust* (Hart Publishing).

—— (2004) 'Chancery Reform and Law Reform' 22 *Law and History Review* 601.

—— (2009a) 'Transplantation and Mutation in Anglo-American Trust Law' 10 *Theoretical Inquiries in Law* 355.

—— (2009b) 'Fiduciary Investment in the Shadow of Financial Crisis – Was Lord Eldon Right?' 3 *Journal of Equity* 219.

—— (2011) 'As If – Accountability and Counterfactual Trust' 91 *Boston University Law Review* 973.

—— (2014) 'Financial Crisis and the Decline of Fiduciary Law' in Morris and Vines (eds), *Capital Failure: Rebuilding Trust in Financial Services* (Oxford University Press).

Glister, J (2014) 'Breach of Trust and Consequential Loss' 8 *Journal of Equity* 235.

Goode, R (2018) *Fundamental Concepts of Commercial Law* (Oxford University Press).

Grower, J (2021) 'Explaining Informal Trusts of Land' *Conveyancer & Property Lawyer* 326.

Hackney, J (1981) 'The Politics of the Chancery' 34 *Current Legal Problems* 113.

—— (1987) *Understanding Equity and Trusts* (Fontana).

—— (2001) 'Snell's Equity' 117 *Law Quarterly Review* 150.

Harding, M (2020) 'Independence and Accountability in the Charity Sector' in Picton and Sigafoos (eds), *Debates in Charity Law* (Hart Publishing).

Harrington, B (2020) *Capital Without Borders: Wealth Managers and the One Percent* (Harvard University Press).

Ho, L (2013) 'Trusts: The Essentials' in Smith (ed), *The Worlds of the Trust* (Cambridge University Press).

—— (2016) 'An Account of Accounts' 28 *Singapore Academy of Law Journal* 849.

—— (2018) '"Breaking Bad": Settlors' Reserved Powers' in Nolan, Low and Tang (eds), *Trusts and Modern Wealth Management* (Cambridge University Press).

Ho, L and Nolan, R (2020) 'The Performance Interest in the Law of Trusts' 136 *Law Quarterly Review* 402.

Hofri-Winogradow, AS (2015) 'The Stripping of the Trust: A Study in Legal Evolution' 65 *University of Toronto Law Journal* 1.

Honoré, AM (1961) 'Ownership' in Guest (ed), *Oxford Essays in Jurisprudence* (Oxford University Press).

Jones, G (1969) *History of the Law of Charity 1532–1837* (Cambridge University Press).

Langbein, JH (1995) 'The Contractarian Basis of the Law of Trusts' 105 *Yale Law Journal* 625.

—— (1996) 'The Uniform Prudent Investor Act and the Future of Trust Investing' 81 *Iowa Law Review* 641.

—— (1997) 'The Secret Life of the Trust: The Trust as an Instrument of Commerce' 107 *Yale Law Journal* 165.

—— (2004) 'Rise of the Management Trust' 143 *Trusts & Estates* 52.

—— (2005) 'Questioning the Trust Law Duty of Loyalty: Sole Interest or Best Interest?' 114 *Yale Law Journal* 929.

Law Commission (2014) 'Fiduciary Duties of Investment Intermediaries' (Law Com No 350).

—— (2020) 'Intermediated Securities: Who Owns Your Shares? A Scoping Paper'.

Lewis, M (2011) *The Big Short* (Penguin).

Liew, YK (2017) *Rationalising Constructive Trusts* (Hart Publishing).

Liew, YK and Mitchell, C (2017) 'The Creation of Express Trusts' 11 *Journal of Equity* 133.

Lobban, M (2004) 'Preparing for Fusion: Reforming the Nineteenth-Century Court of Chancery, Parts I and II' 22 *Law and History Review* 389, 565.

Low, K (2021) 'Trusts of Cryptoassets' 34 *Trusts Law International* 191.

Lowenstein, R (2001) *When Genius Failed: The Rise and Fall of Long Term Capital Management* (Fourth Estate).

Lowrey, A (2021) 'Could Index Funds be "Worse than Marxism"?' *The Atlantic*, April 5 2021.

Maitland, FW (1905) 'Trust and Corporation', reprinted in Runciman and Ryan (eds), *Maitland: State, Trust and Corporation* (Cambridge University Press, 2003).

—— (1936) *Equity: A Course of Lectures* (Cambridge University Press).

Malkiel, BG (2020) *A Random Walk Down Wall Street* (WW Norton & Co).

Matthews, P (1996) 'The New Trust: Obligations Without Rights?' in Oakley (ed), *Trends in Contemporary Trust Law* (Oxford University Press).

McBride, NJ (2013) 'Restitution for Wrongs' in Mitchell and Swadling (eds), *The Restatement Third: Restitution and Unjust Enrichment* (Hart Publishing).

—— (2017) *Key Ideas in Contract Law* (Hart Publishing).

—— (2018) 'The Future of Clean Hands' in Davies, Douglas and Goudkamp (eds), *Defences in Equity* (Hart Publishing).

—— (2019) *The Humanity of Private Law, Part I: Explanation* (Hart Publishing).

—— (2020) *The Humanity of Private Law, Part II: Evaluation* (Hart Publishing).

McFarlane, B (2004) 'Constructive Trusts Arising on a Receipt of Property *Sub Conditione*' 120 *Law Quarterly Review* 667.

—— (2010) 'The Centrality of Constructive and Resulting Trusts' in Mitchell (ed), *Constructive and Resulting Trusts* (Hart Publishing).

McFarlane, B and Stevens, R (2010) 'The Nature of Equitable Property' 4 *Journal of Equity* 1.

Meagher, RP, Gummow, WMC, and Lehane, JRF (1992) *Equity: Doctrines & Remedies*, 3rd edn (Butterworths).

—— (2014), *Meagher, Gummow and Lehane's Equity: Doctrines & Remedies*, 5th edn (eds Heydon, Leeming and Turner) (LexisNexis Butterworths).

Mee, J (2017) 'The Past, Present, and Future of Resulting Trusts' 70 *Current Legal Problems* 189.

Millett, PJ (1985) 'The *Quistclose* Trust: Who Can Enforce It?' 101 *Law Quarterly Review* 269.

—— (2008) 'Equity's Place in the Law of Commerce' 114 *Law Quarterly Review* 214.

—— (2011) 'The *Quistclose* Trust – A Reply' 17 *Trusts & Trustees* 7.

—— (2012) 'Bribes and Secret Commissions Again' 71 *Cambridge Law Journal* 583.

—— (2015) 'The Common Lawyer and the Equity Practitioner' 6 *UK Supreme Court Yearbook* 193.

Mitchell, C (2002) 'Assistance' in Birks and Pretto (eds), *Breach of Trust* (Hart Publishing).

—— (2013) 'Equitable Compensation for Breach of Fiduciary Duty' 66 *Current Legal Problems* 307.

—— (2014) 'Stewardship of Property and Liability to Account' *Conveyancer & Property Lawyer* 215.

—— (2020) 'Charitable Endowment and Social Change: Cy-Près Orders and Schemes 1837–1901' 41 *The Journal of Legal History* 29.

Mitchell, C and Watterson, S (2009) 'Remedies for Knowing Receipt' in Mitchell (ed), *Constructive and Resulting Trusts* (Hart Publishing).

Moffat, G (2020) *Moffat's Trusts Law*, 7th edn (eds Garton, Probert and Bean) (Cambridge University Press).

Molloy, T (2009) 'I Am a Trustee. I Can't Make Head or Tail of the Black-Scholes Formula. Am I at Risk?' 15 *Trusts & Trustees* 524.

Murphy, R (2017) *Dirty Secrets: How Tax Havens Destroy the Economy* (Verso).

Nicholls, D (1998) 'Knowing Receipt: The Need for a New Landmark' in Cornish, Nolan, O'Sullivan and Virgo (eds), *Restitution: Past, Present and Future* (Hart Publishing).

—— (2014) 'Trustees and Their Broader Community: Where Duty, Morality and Ethics Converge' 9 *Trusts Law International* 71.

Noe, T and Young, HP (2014) 'The Limits to Compensation in the Financial Sector' in Morris and Vines (eds), *Capital Failure: Rebuilding Trust in Financial Services* (Oxford University Press).

Noyes, CR (1936) *The Institution of Property* (Longman Publishing).

Oakley, AJ (1997) *Constructive Trusts*, 3rd edn (Sweet & Maxwell).

Obermayer, B and Obermaier, F (2017) *The Panama Papers* (Oneworld Publications).

Parkinson, P (2002) 'Reconceptualising the Express Trust' 61 *Cambridge Law Journal* 657.

Penner, JE (2014) 'Purposes and Rights in the Common Law of Trusts' 48 *Revue Juridique Themis* 579.

—— (2020) 'Private Law Offices' 70 (Supplement 2) *University of Toronto Law Journal* 299.

—— (2022) *The Law of Trusts*, 12th edn (Oxford University Press).

Rudden, B (1994) 'Things as Thing and Things as Wealth' 14 *Oxford Journal of Legal Studies* 81.

Samet, I (2008) 'Guarding the Fiduciary's Conscience: A Justification of a Stringent Profit-Stripping Rule' 28 *Oxford Journal of Legal Studies* 763.

—— (2018) *Equity: Conscience Goes to Market* (Oxford University Press).

Shaxson, N (2012) *Treasure Islands: Tax Havens and the Men Who Stole the World* (Vintage).

—— (2019) *The Finance Curse: How Global Finance is Making Us All Poorer* (Vintage).

Smith, L (1999) 'Constructive Trusts and Constructive Trustees' 58 *Cambridge Law Journal* 294.

—— (2000) 'Unjust Enrichment, Property, and the Structure of Trusts' 116 *Law Quarterly Review* 412.

—— (2013) 'Stateless Trusts' in Smith (ed), *The Worlds of the Trust* (Cambridge University Press).

—— (2014) 'Fiduciary Relationships: Ensuring the Loyal Exercise of Judgment on Behalf of Another' 130 *Law Quarterly Review* 608.

—— (2017) 'Massively Discretionary Trusts' 70 *Current Legal Problems* 17.

—— (2018) 'Give the People What They Want? The Onshoring of the Offshore' 103 *Iowa Law Review* 2155.

Smolyansky, M (2010) 'Reining in the *Quistclose* Trust' 16 *Trusts & Trustees* 558.

St Germain, C (1771) *Doctor and Student: Dialogues Between a Doctor of Divinity and a Student of the Common Law*, 16th edn (J Worrall).

Sterk, SE (1999) 'Asset Protection Trusts: Trust Law's Race to the Bottom?' 85 *Cornell Law Review* 1035.

Stevens, R (2008) 'Contract Lite' (UCL inaugural lecture, Nov 20 2008).

—— (2012) 'When and Why Does Unjustified Enrichment Justify the Recognition of Proprietary Rights?' 92 *Boston University LR* 919.

—— (2017) 'Floating Trusts' in Davies and Penner (eds), *Equity, Trusts and Commerce* (Hart Publishing).

Story, J (1920) *Commentaries on Equity Jurisprudence*, 3rd edn (Sweet & Maxwell).

Swadling, W (1996) 'A New Role for Resulting Trusts?' 16 *Legal Studies* 110.

—— (2004) 'Orthodoxy' in Swadling (ed), *The Quistclose Trust: Critical Essays* (Hart Publishing).

—— (2008) 'Explaining Resulting Trusts' 124 *Law Quarterly Review* 72.

—— (2010) 'The Nature of the Trust in *Rochefoucauld v Boustead*' in Mitchell (ed), *Constructive and Resulting Trusts* (Hart Publishing).

—— (2011) 'The Fiction of the Constructive Trust' 64 *Current Legal Problems* 399.

—— (2013a) 'Legislating in Vain' in Burrows (ed), *Judge and Jurist: Essays in Memory of Lord Rodger of Earlsferry* (Oxford University Press).

—— (2013b) 'Property: General Principles' in Burrows (ed), *English Private Law*, 3rd edn (Oxford University Press).

—— (2016) 'Trust and Ownership: A Common Law Perspective' 6 *European Review of Private Law* 951.

—— (2019a) 'In Defence of Formalism' in Robertson and Goudkamp (eds), *Form and Substance in the Law of Obligations* (Hart Publishing).

—— (2019b) 'The Nature of "Knowing Receipt"' in Davies and Penner (eds), *Equity, Trusts and Commerce* (Hart Publishing).

Turner, PG (2012) 'Understanding the Constructive Trust between Vendor and Purchaser' 128 *Law Quarterly Review* 582.

Watson, JA (2016) *The Duty to Account: Development and Principles* (Federation Press).

Whitehead, P (1985) *The Writing on the Wall: Britain in the Seventies* (Michael Joseph Ltd).

Wilde, D (2020) 'The Three Certainties Required to Declare a Trust – or Is It Four? "Distributional Certainty"' 79 *Cambridge Law Journal* 349.

——— (2022) 'Trusts of Imperfect Obligation' 28 *Trusts & Trustees* 298.

Worthington, S (2013) 'Fiduciary Duties and Proprietary Remedies: Addressing the Failure of Equitable Formulae' 72 *Cambridge Law Journal* 720.

Willoughby, P (2002) *Misplaced Trust*, 2nd edn (ed Wadham) (Gostick Hall Publications).

World Bank, The (2011) *The Puppet Masters: How the Corrupt Use Legal Structures to Hide Stolen Assets and What to Do About It* (eds Does de Willebois, Halter, Harrison, Park and Sharman) (The International Bank for Reconstruction and Development/The World Bank).

Zhang, R (2022) 'Principal Forms of Commercial Trusts in the UK and the Rethinking of Traditional Approaches' 28 *Trusts & Trustees* 787.

Zucman, G (2015) *The Hidden Wealth of Nations* (University of Chicago Press).

TABLE OF CASES

Printed in the USA
CPSIA information can be obtained
at www.ICGtesting.com
LVHW011737230923
759042LV00003B/603

9 781509 938698